D0876385

WITHDRAWN

A ROOM OF ONE'S OWN

Women Writers and the Politics of Creativity

TWAYNE'S MASTERWORK STUDIES

Robert Lecker, General Editor

A ROOM OF ONE'S OWN

Women Writers and the Politics of Creativity

Ellen Bayuk Rosenman

TWAYNE PUBLISHERS • NEW YORK
Maxwell Macmillan Canada • Toronto
Maxwell Macmillan International • New York Oxford Singapore Sydney

Twayne's Masterwork Studies No. 151

A Room of One's Own
Ellen Bayuk Rosenman

Copyright © 1995 by Twayne Publishers
All rights reserved. No part of this book may be reproduced or transmitted in any form
or by any means, electronic or mechanical, including photocopying, recording, or by
any information storage and retrieval system, without permission in writing from the
Publisher.

Twayne Publishers   Maxwell Macmillan Canada, Inc.
Macmillan Publishing Company   1200 Eglinton Avenue East
866 Third Avenue   Suite 200
New York, New York 10022   Don Mills, Ontario M3C 3N1

Library of Congress Cataloging-in-Publication Data

Rosenman, Ellen Bayuk.
    A room of one's own : women writers and the politics of creativity / Ellen Bayuk
Rosenman.
        p. cm.—(Twayne's masterwork studies ; 151)
    Includes bibliographical references and index.
    ISBN 0-8057-8374-1—ISBN 0-8057-8594-9 (pbk.)
    1. Woolf, Virginia, 1882–1941—Political and social views. 2. Feminism and litera-
ture—England—History—20th century. 3. Women and literature—England—
History—20th century. 4. Woolf, Virginia, 1882–1941. Room of one's own. 5.
Creativity—Political aspects. 6. Authorship—Sex differences. 7. Feminism and litera-
ture. 8. Women and literature. I. Title. II. Series.
PR6045.O72Z86734   1994
823'.912—dc20   94-25607
                                                                         CIP

The paper used in this publication meets the minimum requirements of American
National Standard for Information Sciences—Permanence of Paper for Printed Library
Materials. ANSI Z39.48-1984.∞ ™

10 9 8 7 6 5 4 3 2 1 (alk. paper)
10 9 8 7 6 5 4 3 2 1 (pbk.: alk. paper)

Printed in the United States of America.

Contents

Note on the References and Acknowledgments

I have used the most recent paperback edition of *A Room of One's Own*, with an introduction by the novelist Mary Gordon (New York: Harcourt, Brace, Jovanovich, 1981). The photograph of Virginia Woolf, taken in 1928 by Harlingue-Viollet, is reproduced with permission of the Collection Roget-Viollet. I want to thank my indefatigable research assistant, Kakie Urch, who found everything, and the University of Kentucky for funding her work.

Virginia Woolf in 1928.
Photo by Harlingue-Viollet.

Chronology: Virginia Woolf's Life and Works

1882	Adeline Virginia Stephen born 25 January in London at 22 Hyde Park Gate, the third child of Leslie and Julia Duckworth Stephen (Vanessa and Thoby are siblings). Adrian is born a year later. The family also includes Laura, Leslie Stephen's retarded daughter from a previous marriage, and Stella, Gerald, and George, the children of Julia from a previous marriage. Both of these marriages ended with the death of the spouse.
ca. 1888	Half-brother Gerald molests Virginia.
1895	Mother dies. Virginia experiences her first mental breakdown.
1897	Half-sister Stella marries Jack Hills in April, develops an infection on their honeymoon, and dies in July.
1899	Thoby enters Cambridge. Virginia studies Latin at home with Janet Case.
1904	Father dies; sexual advances of half-brother George precipitate Virginia's second breakdown, which includes a suicide attempt. Virginia, Vanessa, Thoby, and Adrian move to 46 Gordon Square in Bloomsbury. Virginia publishes her first review in the *Guardian*.
1905	Beginning of the Bloomsbury Group: Thoby's friends from Cambridge start their visits. Virginia lectures at Morley College, an institute for working men and women.
1906	Virginia, Vanessa, and Thoby visit Greece. Thoby and Vanessa catch typhoid; Thoby dies.
1907	Begins work on her first novel, now titled *Melymbrosia*; later published as *The Voyage Out*. Vanessa marries Clive Bell, one of Thoby's friends from Cambridge. Virginia and Adrian move to 29 Fitzroy Square, also in Bloomsbury. First major public demonstrations by Women's Social and Political Union, the

suffrage organization led by Emmeline and Christabel Pankhurst, also known as the suffragettes.

1909   Lytton Strachey, another friend of Thoby's, proposes to Virginia. She accepts, but he retracts his offer shortly thereafter. They remain close friends. First hunger strike by suffrage workers in prison.

1910   Works for suffrage organization (probably the People's Suffrage Federation) at the suggestion of her Latin tutor Janet Case. "Black Friday" in London, when police and bystanders sexually assault suffragettes. The first Post-Impressionist Exhibition, organized by Roger Fry. The art of Cézanne and others proves controversial, and Fry becomes a spokesperson for avant-garde art, with the support of the Bloomsbury Group.

1911   Virginia and Adrian move to 38 Brunswick Square with John Maynard Keynes, Duncan Grant, and Leonard Woolf.

1912   Marries Leonard Woolf after much indecision.

1913   Begins working for Women's Co-operative Guild, a moderate suffrage organization. Completes *The Voyage Out*, which is to be published by her half-brother Gerald. Probably because of anxieties about her manuscript and about marriage, she experiences her third and most severe mental breakdown to date. Again, she attempts suicide. This breakdown lasts for three years.

1914   World War I begins.

1917   Virginia and Leonard Woolf found the Hogarth Press, named after Hogarth House, where they live in Richmond. Originally a simple hand-press run as a hobby, it grows into a significant commercial press that publishes many of the most important writers of the day. Their first publication is a book of two short stories, one by Leonard and one by Virginia. Writes reviews for the *Times of London Literary Supplement*.

1918   World War I ends. Woolf begins work on her second novel, *Night and Day*. Suffrage is granted to women over the age of 30 who are householders or the wives of householders—a little more than half the adult female population.

1919   *Night and Day* is published by Gerald Duckworth. The Woolfs buy Monk's House in Rodmell, Sussex, a country home to which they retreat frequently.

1920   Woolf begins her exchange with Desmond MacCarthy on "The Intellectual Status of Women" in the *New Statesman*, sowing the seeds for *A Room of One's Own*.

1922	*Jacob's Room* published by Hogarth Press. Woolf hereafter publishes all her own novels in England. James Joyce's *Ulysses* and T. S. Eliot's *The Waste Land* also appear.
1924	The Woolfs move to 52 Tavistock Square, which will remain their London address for over a decade.
1925	Publishes the novel *Mrs. Dalloway* and the collection of essays *The Common Reader*. Begins working on *To the Lighthouse*. Becomes acquainted with Vita Sackville-West, aristocratic wife of diplomat Harold Nicolson. The two begin an affair, probably with the knowledge of their husbands, which does not undermine either marriage.
1927	Publishes *To the Lighthouse* and begins planning *The Jessemy Brides*, which will become *Orlando*.
1928	Publishes *Orlando*, dedicated to Vita Sackville-West. The novel is a fantasy of the life of a young boy in Elizabethan England who lives until the present day and changes into a woman midway through his life. Sackville-West is the model for this character, and Woolf includes photographs of Sackville-West in the novel. Women achieve full suffrage. Woolf delivers lectures at the two Cambridge women's colleges, Newnham and Girton, that will become *A Room of One's Own*. The obscenity trial begins for *The Well of Loneliness*, a lesbian novel by Radclyffe Hall that Woolf is prepared to defend. The case is alluded to in *A Room of One's Own*.
1929	Publishes *A Room of One's Own* and the essay "Women and Fiction," both taken from the Cambridge talks. Begins work on a novel that she calls *The Moths* and later renames *The Waves*.
1931	Publishes *The Waves*.
1932	Publishes the collection of essays *The Second Common Reader*. Begins to think about a sequel to *A Room of One's Own* that will intersperse fiction and nonfiction. It is tentatively titled *The Pargiters*, after the fictitious multigenerational family about whom Woolf plans to write. An early draft includes a lengthy version of what will eventually become the essay "Professions for Women." Cambridge University invites her to deliver the prestigious Clark Lectures on literature, which her father gave in the nineteenth century. She declines. Lytton Strachey dies.
1933	Publishes *Flush*, a novel telling the story of the relationship between Elizabeth Barrett and Robert Browning, told from the point of view of Barrett's dog Flush.

1935	The London Library Committee rejects Woolf as a potential member because "ladies are quite impossible."
1936	Finally finishes *The Years*, having removed the nonfiction chapters. Begins to work this material into the essay *Three Guineas*. The Spanish Civil War begins.
1937	*The Years* appears; it is Woolf's first best-seller. Her beloved nephew Julian, an ambulance driver, is killed in the Spanish Civil War.
1938	Publishes *Three Guineas*, a long essay connecting sexism, classism, and fascism. It is violently attacked as elitist by Q. D. Leavis in the journal *Scrutiny*, which has become a focal point for a new generation of professional critics who wish to supplant the bellelettrist tradition of Bloomsbury.
1939	The Woolfs move to Monk's House, paying brief visits to London, where they now live at 37 Mecklenburgh Square. England declares war on Germany.
1940	Woolf publishes *Roger Fry*, a biography of her friend the artist and critic. Battle of Britain. The Woolfs' London home is severely bombed; they stockpile morphine, planning to commit suicide in the event of a German invasion. Because Leonard is Jewish and both are left-wing intellectuals, they expect to be on Hitler's death list.
1941	Experiences fourth mental breakdown, probably caused or intensified by her fear about the war. Begins hearing voices. Puts stones in her pockets and drowns herself in the Ouse River, in Sussex. Her novel *Between the Acts* is published posthumously.

LITERARY AND
HISTORICAL CONTEXT

1

Virginia Woolf and Her World

Adeline Virginia Stephen was born on 25 January 1882, the third child of Sir Leslie Stephen and Julia Duckworth Stephen. Along with her seven siblings—including three children from her mother's previous marriage—she grew up in a large house at Hyde Park Gate, London.

These simple facts speak volumes about the cultural and historical milieu into which Woolf was born. Sometimes thought of as a quintessentially modernist writer, Woolf came of age in an environment that was emphatically Victorian. Queen Victoria had nearly 20 years left in her reign when Woolf was born. Woolf's parents were the sort of eminent Victorians that her friend Lytton Strachey brought to life and demystified in his book of that title. One of the foremost essayists and intellectuals of his day, her father edited the prestigious *Cornhill Magazine* and was commissioned to edit the first *Dictionary of National Biography*, a daunting task that consumed an entire decade of his life. Her mother was a celebrated beauty who posed for Edward Burne-Jones's painting *The Annunciation* and for the photographs of her famous aunt, Julia Margaret Cameron. Woolf was born into an intellectual and artistic circle that included the novelists Henry James and George Meredith; she was related to William Makepeace Thackeray through her father's first marriage. In many ways, she stood at the center of Victorian culture.

Nevertheless, Woolf also felt uneasy in this world. However much an insider her pedigree made her, Victorian beliefs about gender excluded her as well. The belief in separate spheres strictly limited the kinds of experience and power available to women. According to Victorian thought, society was divided into two worlds: the public world of commerce, in which competition, selfishness, and materialistic values ruled, and the private world of the home, which provided comfort, companionship, and spiritual renewal. Men would leave the home every morning, enter the hurly-burly of the marketplace, and return home in the evening to be cleansed of the contamination of public, mercantile life. A series of sex-linked characteristics grew from this idea: men are active, competitive, productive; women are passive, unselfish, decorative. God and nature, it was argued, ordained such a division of human traits. While much social commentary presented the separate spheres as complementary, they were clearly hierarchical. By any objective measure, men simply had more power than women, and masculine traits and activities were more highly valued.

Despite her father's free-thinking intellectual habits and her mother's strength of character, these beliefs influenced Woolf's family. While she was encouraged to read, study, and think for herself, she was also required to sit politely through the stultifying visits that were an obligatory part of woman's work. Her "tea-table training," as she called it, brought her up to hide her strength and intellectual independence beneath a facade of deferential feminine charm.[1] Woolf was hardly a natural. She remembered stunning an aristocratic gathering with the mention of Plato. "They're not used to young women saying *anything*—," her half-brother whispered, mortified.[2] The roles of her parents reflected these assumptions as well. Her father's demanding, irascible behavior, she felt, was a by-product of male privilege, made acceptable by the fact that men were expected to assert themselves and that Woolf's mother could always be depended on to smooth the ruffled feathers of whomever Leslie Stephen offended.

The most disturbing extension of this theory of sex roles was the sexual abuse that Woolf experienced at the hands of George and Gerald Duckworth, her half-brothers from her mother's first marriage. She remembered Gerald exploring her body when she was only six, and George fondling her 15 years later, when her father was dying of cancer. The nineteenth-century belief that men could not be expected to control their sexual desires, coupled with male social power and a general refusal to discuss sexual matters, left the young Woolf defenseless against their advances. Her sense of the vulnerability of the female body, grounded in an objective understanding of social structure, also owes much to her childhood traumas. Against these Victorian beliefs about gender, Woolf fought much of her life. *A Room of One's Own* is one of her first concerted attempts to create a counter-theory to Victorian sex roles.

Woolf burst free of this world after her parents' death, when she moved with her sister Vanessa and her brothers Thoby and Adrian to 46 Gordon Square, in an area of London called Bloomsbury. The year was 1904; she was 22 years old and recovering from a mental breakdown. The move across London—a matter of a few miles—remade her as an independent, unconventional person. The name "Bloomsbury" has become synonymous with the free-wheeling intellectual, artistic, and sexual circle in which Woolf declared her independence from Victorian social codes. Several years later and at a different Bloomsbury address she lived with her brother Adrian and three of her brother's Cambridge friends—one of whom, Leonard Woolf, she married in 1912. A more dramatic departure from her past would be hard to imagaine. Henry James, for one, was shocked that "Leslie's daughters" would have chosen such living arrangements.[3]

In these years, when she was nobody's daughter and nobody's wife, Woolf entered into a community composed of her siblings and her brother Thoby's friends from Cambridge. The Bloomsbury Group provided Woolf with a precious commodity: intellectual conversation. No one cared what she wore or how gracefully she poured tea; they wanted to hear her opinion of Plato and scores of other serious matters. She remembered with pleasure the transition from her half-brother's social advice—"You must learn to do your hair"—to the intellectual camaraderie of Bloomsbury—"I must say you made your point rather well" (191). Conventional wisdom was scorned; carefully argued and original positions on art and ethics dominated their evenings. Sexual relations, too, pushed the boundaries of Victorian propriety, as Bloomsbury's members paired off in various combinations, both heterosexual and homosexual. Woolf took a dramatic step out of the nineteenth century when she entered this new home.

While she must have learned much from these university-educated men, she maintained a critical perspective on their learning as well, writing an incisive parody of a collection of poems by the Cambridge men called, pretentiously, *Euphrosyne* (one of the three Graces in Greek mythology). Neither Woolf nor her sister Vanessa, studying to be an artist, allowed herself to be overwhelmed by the superior formal training of their male companions. One of their circle, Duncan Grant (with whom Vanessa lived for much of her adult life) reported: "These . . . young men found to their amazement that they could be shocked by the boldness and skepticism of two young women."[4] Although there has been much debate, even among its members, about whether the Bloomsbury Group should be called a group at all, it functioned for Woolf as a solid if shifting community, perhaps even a second family, that nurtured in her a sense of intellectual confidence and freedom. Although several members of this community might fairly be called "misogynist" in their publicly expressed opinions, she remembers the early days of their conversations as a liberating era in which her intellectual abilities were taken absolutely seriously and her tea-table training in femininity meant absolutely nothing.

When Woolf completed her first novel in 1913, she entered another experimental world—that of literary modernism. James Joyce's *Dubliners* was published in 1914, D. H. Lawrence's *The Rainbow* in 1915, T. S. Eliot's *The Love Song of J. Alfred Prufrock* in 1915. These writers continued to form the context for one another's work through the 1920s. Woolf was part of the literary explosion of 1922, in which Joyce's *Ulysses*, Eliot's *The Waste Land*, and her own *Jacob's Room* were published (in fact, the Hogarth Press, which Woolf owned and ran with her husband, published a hand-printed edition of

The Waste Land in 1923). These writers rejected conventional plot and character and emphasized instead states of mind, rendered in a fluid, associative mode that has become known as "stream of consciousness." Along with Woolf's fiction, the technique of *A Room of One's Own* owes much to these modernist experiments.

Along with this cultural background *A Room of One's Own* needs to be understood in the context of contemporary (to Woolf) feminism, particularly the suffrage movement. Twentieth-century suffragist activity was the culmination of many decades of social protest by women, directed at a range of social laws and practices ranging from restrictions on women's education to the enforced treatment of prostitutes for venereal disease. Not surprisingly, diverse assumptions characterized these efforts, and sometimes collided. Some believed that women deserved enfranchisement on the basis of their equality with men as rational beings, as Mary Wollstonecraft argued over a century before in *A Vindication of the Rights of Women*. Others thought women should stake their claim to public participation on the basis of their difference from men, as the more virtuous, selfless, and cooperative sex, as much Victorian ideology asserted. Thus the modern suffrage movement kept alive a legacy of questions about woman's nature—questions Woolf inherited.

By 1903, with the founding of Women's Social and Political Union by Emmeline and Christabel Pankhurst, most of women's political energy was concentrated into the fight for the vote. Using "'sensational public protest'" as its strategy, the WSPU gained widespread attention from its inception until the onset of World War I.[5] Not only its tactics but the male backlash against it placed sexual politics vividly in the public eye. By 1910 the suffragettes—as this militant wing of the movement was called—turned to hunger strikes to protest their imprisonment. They were brutally force-fed and sometimes assaulted in their cells. In an infamous incident in 1910, called "Black Friday," suffragettes who were marching on Parliament were sexually attacked by police. Such incidents were widely reported in the press, and they commanded the sympathy of moderate women who had never engaged in politics before. Moreover, this violent and abusive backlash dramatized the very imbalance of power between the sexes, which suffrage workers protested; in a sense, it confirmed their argument that women were oppressed, second-class citizens in their own country. After a hiatus of political activity during the war, female householders (or wives of householders) over age 30 won suffrage in 1918. Full women's suffrage followed in 1928.

For Virginia Woolf, a woman in her twenties who had begun to live an independent life, the suffrage movement was a compelling project. About the time when she moved to Bloomsbury she recorded her first interest in women's history. In 1910 she wrote to her Latin tutor Janet Case to volunteer for the Adult Suffragists, a moderate wing of the suffrage movement. Woolf's letter reflects a strong sense of injustice along with a lack of experience in—and perhaps a certain discomfort with—direct political action. Nevertheless, Woolf worked for this organization, as she did for the Women's Co-operative Guild later in her life, as a way of connecting her private beliefs to the public world. It seems likely, too, that the violent treatment of the suffragettes spoke to her in direct and personal ways. In periods of mental stress Woolf had difficulty eating and, if not exactly force-fed, was coerced into eating against her will. And the molestation of the suffragettes may have resonated with her own childhood experience of sexual abuse.

The suffrage movement may have affected Woolf in another way. Some recent critics have suggested that literary modernism itself was shaped by a reaction against feminist agitation. Responding anxiously to the prospect of new sex roles as well as a more generalized sense of cultural crisis, "modernist formulations of societal breakdown consistently employed imagery of male impotence and female potency," Sandra Gilbert and Susan Gubar suggest.[6] Woolf would certainly have been interested in this idea, given her prediction in A Room of One's Own that "Elizabethan literature would have been very different from what it is if the woman's movement had begun in the sixteenth century and not in the nineteenth" (101). As A Room of One's Own repeatedly suggests, Woolf lived in a world of male antagonism, perhaps because rather than in spite of the success of suffrage agitation. Woolf writes, "The history of men's opposition to women's emancipation is more interesting perhaps than the story of that emancipation itself" (55). Much of A Room of One's Own recounts that history, which continues to what for Woolf was the present day. Thus Woolf wrote both with and against the grain of modernism, participating in its technical experiments but resisting its misogyny.

In any case, Woolf's emerging interest in women's place in society coincided with the intensification of suffrage activity. And while biographers generally stress her personal acquaintance with influential male figures such as Henry James and John Maynard Keynes, she also enjoyed close friendships with several pioneering feminists, such as Ray Strachey and Margaret Llewellyn Davies. To Davies, whom she addressed as "Dearest Margaret," she writes in 1916, "I become steadily more feminist, owing to the *Times*" and its coverage of the war.[7] Although Woolf disavows the word "feminist" in her essay *Three Guineas* (albeit in a characteristically ironic way) and argues in *A Room of One's Own* that the vote was of secondary importance to the right to enter the professions, she remained committed to women's equality throughout her life. Although she has been characterized as apolitical by older critics and biographers, her writing maintains an unwavering interest in sexual politics. However active or inactive she was in organized politics—and the point continues to be debated—there is no doubt that she was a political thinker and that her most fervent political commitment was to women and their rights.

2

The Importance of *A Room of One's Own*

"But my 'book' isn't a book—its only talks to girls," Virginia Woolf wrote, with tongue in cheek, about *A Room of One's Own*.[1] The adulation that has been heaped on Woolf's essay tells a very different story. Looking back on her discovery of *A Room of One's Own*, the novelist Margaret Drabble writes, "I read it with mounting excitement and enthusiasm. . . . A more militant, firm, concerted attack on women's subjection would be hard to find. I could hardly believe that a woman from her background . . . could speak so relevantly to my own condition."[2] From the time of the book's publication to today, many other readers have echoed Drabble's assessment. Despite the ways in which Woolf's background might alienate her readers—her class privilege, her intellectual elitism, her experimental aesthetic philosophy, the distance between her era and our own—*A Room of One's Own* has managed to reach across boundaries with its powerful message. For a book that is not a book but "only talks to girls," *A Room of One's Own* has done very well.

The title, with its theme of autonomy and independence, has become part of our modern cultural vocabulary, testifying to the essay's widespread influence. If imitation is the sincerest form of flattery, then *A Room of One's Own* is surely one of the most flattered books in history. One might almost say that it has spawned a cottage industry of self-conscious inheritance, as an impressive array of enterprises has appropriated and remade its title. One of the earliest "second-wave" (that is, postsuffrage) works of literary criticism, published in 1977, was Elaine Showalter's *A Literature of Their Own*. A modern journal of criticism calls itself *A Room of One's Own*. Similar titles include "A Life of One's Own" (an article about Georges Sand), "A Quest of One's Own" (about Doris Lessing), "Words of One's Own" (about Woolf and Adrienne Rich), *A Voice of One's Own* (a collection of fiction by women), "An Income of One's Own" (about money and *Moll Flanders*) "A Criticism of *His* Own" (about male feminist critics; italics mine), "A Book of One's Own" (about diaries), "A Life of One's Own" (about Onerva, a Finnish woman writer), "A Language of One's Own" (about *Mrs. Dalloway*), and—surely one Woolf would not have anticipated—"An Asteroid of One's Own" (about women science fiction writers of the Soviet Union). Twice in the past 10 years authors have titled their essays "A Womb of One's Own." And this list is by no means exhaustive. The famous "Chloe liked Olivia" passage has also inspired appropriation: a novel by Bell Gale Chevigny was called *Chloe and Olivia*, and Two Nice Girls, a lesbian rock band from Texas, titled their 1993 album *Chloe Liked Olivia*, quoting from *A Room of One's Own* in the liner notes. Like quotations from Shakespeare, Woolf's famous phrases have passed into the realm of idiom, familiar and resonant in any number of contexts and uses.

The importance of the work itself is difficult to overestimate. It was the first literary history of women writers and the first theory of literary inheritance in which gender was the central category. These facts alone would assure its historical importance. But Woolf's essay is much more than a historical landmark, although it is difficult to analyze precisely the uncanny symbiosis between this essay, published in 1929, and the various manifestations of modern feminism that originated in the early to mid-1970s. What is perhaps most remarkable is the way in which *A Room of One's Own* has served the needs of various strains of feminist criticism, not all of them compatible with each other. Conventionally, we explain such a phenomenon as evidence of

11

the work's innate and timeless truth, speaking to all people at all times. This is an assumption that helps us to construct a piece of literature as a "masterwork." Such an argument would be inappropriate to *A Room of One's Own*, however, for Woolf's essay insists on the time-bound and contextual nature of literary achievement. Instead, it may be worthwhile to consider some more specific reasons that the essay has gained its reputation as the most single important work of feminist literary criticism.

When feminist criticism emerged in the 1970s *A Room of One's Own* was one of the few works of its sort in print. Although it is literary and associative rather than abstract and philosophical, it functioned then—as it does now—as a *theory* of women's literature. It laid out general ideas and issues through which the lives and works of women writers might profitably be read. Woolf did not offer extended readings of individual literary works; instead she speculated about why and how women wrote as they did, which was infinitely more valuable to twentieth-century critics who were attempting to map out the new terrain of women's literature.

Another reason for the essay's importance is the fame of its author, who has become something of a cult figure. Her extraordinary accomplishments, along with the tragic and sensational aspects of Woolf's biography, have led to divergent constructions of Woolf herself as an ancestor of modern feminism. She has been portrayed as both a "guerrilla fighter in Victorian skirts," leading women against patriarchy and a victim of patriarchy, excluded from patriarchy's privileges and undermined as a confident, independent adult.[3] She has recently been identified as an incest survivor, whose life is reinterpreted in relation to modern testimonies about violence against women.[4] Woolf can serve as the heroine, victim, and survivor, once again depending on the perspective of the reader. Because Woolf has taken on this symbolic importance as a figurehead for women, her works take on an additional interest, particularly one that discusses gender as overtly as *A Room of One's Own*.

It is difficult to assess just how much *A Room of One's Own* directed the interests of modern feminist criticism and how much modern feminist criticism set its own agendas and then found corroboration in Woolf's essay, assuring the essay's continuing importance by finding it useful for preexisting purposes. Perhaps if feminist criticism had taken other forms another work would enjoy the canonical status of *A Room of One's Own*. But there is no doubt that Woolf's essay *has* become a canonical text for the multifaceted feminist literary criticism of the last two decades. *A Room of One's Own* is a sort of primer of feminist concepts: the experience of oppression and victimization, the importance of exclusion and marginality, the existence of a distinctive female voice and subject matter. Even her apparently passing assertion that "we think back through our mothers if we are women" (76) has taken its place at the center of an important thread of feminist thought among studies of mothers and daughters in literature, psychoanalytic theories of female identity that stress the mother-daughter relationship, and philosophical investigations of maternal thinking as a paradigm for ethical human behavior. These modern theories have pursued, or perhaps reinvented, Woolf's intuition that the mother-daughter relationship is a powerful trope for female experience.

One important characteristic of *A Room of One's Own* is that it can accommodate many agendas. Woolf's style is associative and suggestive rather than strictly logical; she throws out ideas at a rapid rate, interweaving a number of different themes and images into any given passage. As criticism has changed, it has still found *A Room of One's Own* a fertile source of ideas and illustrations. The essay does not strive for the strict coherence of a jigsaw puzzle, composed of perfectly interlocking pieces in which no gaps exist and there is nothing left over. We might say that Woolf's essay has proved so durable because it often contradicts itself. The celebration of the feminine style coexists with the valorization of androgyny; the insistence on gender as crucial to women's perspective and experience coexists with a stern admonition to women not to think consciously of their sex. With such divergent assertions *A Room of One's Own* has been impressed into the service of widely divergent points of view. Perhaps one reason that the essay has compelled such interest is that it points to complex issues that are not easily resolved. In tackling them, Woolf left a fruitful series of possibilities for future critics to explore and unravel. Its loose threads are suggestions that we can follow, like strings leading us through a maze, to different and plausible positions depending on our own interests, assumptions, and beliefs.

3

Critical Reception

A Room of One's Own has really had two critical receptions: one when it first appeared and a second 50 or so years later, when it was rediscovered by feminist critics. Like the forgotten women authors whom Woolf exhumes in her essay, *A Room of One's Own* has been buried by one critical establishment only to be recovered by a new set of literary interests and a new generation of readers. It is a "master-work" of relatively recent making. Its newfound canonical status owes everything to changes in critical assumptions and practices. This criti-cal history supports the argument of the essay itself—that what the world calls a "masterpiece" tells us as much about prevailing values as about the work itself.

By 1929, when *A Room of One's Own* was published, Woolf was an established author. She was renowned as a critic: the influential *Times Literary Supplement* called her 1925 collection of literary essays, *The Common Reader*, "the best criticism in English."[1] But she was best known as a novelist, recognized as a self-consciously modern writer who attempted to break with nineteenth-century literary conven-tions. Certainly she was not for every taste. Some critics regularly bemoaned the absence of conventional plots and characters and complained that her meaning and method were unclear. Still, her work was widely praised as original and exciting, beginning with the publication of *Jacob's Room* in 1922. The novels published between *Jacob's Room* and *A Room of One's Own*—*Mrs. Dalloway* (1925), *To the Lighthouse* (1927), and *Orlando* (1928)—were widely regarded as the culmination of her impressionistic and innovative method. Repeatedly praised and damned for her esoteric method and delicate sensibility, Woolf was constructed as a writer preoccupied with states of consciousness at the expense of the outside world and social problems. A representative judgment appeared in *College English*: "There is no struggle [in Woolf's writing], no criticism of society, merely a deft spinning of ideas through the consciousness of her people."[2] She was not perceived as a political writer in any sense. Her friend E. M. Forster's creed of "art for art's sake" seemed to describe Woolf's own philosophy as well.

It is not surprising, then, that *A Room of One's Own* confounded the critics. "What a subject!" exclaimed the *Criterion*.[3] The essay was well-received when it first appeared, although in complicated ways. It was generally treated with a respect that reflected Woolf's public reputation. Nevertheless, what strikes one most about the early reviews is how thoroughly the tone and design of *A Room of One's Own* baffled its first reviewers. Missing its anger and its trenchant irony, most reviewers praised its inoffensive charm. Woolf's intricate, multilayered narrative may have disguised too completely the white-hot anger she felt when she wrote it. Certainly Woolf's image as an experimental, apolitical writer was hard to square with the ideas in *A Room of One's Own*, and may have led critics to concentrate on style, beauty, and tone as more familiar features of her works. Perhaps, too, some critics simply did not want to hear Woolf's passionate indictment of man-made literary history and so heard something else instead. This certainly seems to have been the case with Woolf's old antagonist Arnold Bennett, who applauded her comment that "women are hard on women," completely missing the fact that Woolf presents it as a cliché that she plans to dismantle.[4] Bennett caps his review by criticizing her grammar.

Whatever the reason, *A Room of One's Own* is one of the more misunderstood works of modern literature. A generous sampling of contemporary (to Woolf) criticism suggests the nature of this misunderstanding. According to the *Criterion*, the essay is "composed of delightful *causeries* [chats] on other people's books" and uses its knowledge "so artfully that it seems but a decoration" (510, 509). It is "a delightfully peripeatetic essay,"[5] displaying "inherent taste."[6] It is characterized as "gay,"[7] "enchanting,"[8] "delicious . . . [and] delicately whimsical."[9] The article just quoted also calls it "demure" twice (627, 628). It is easy to see that this is not the usual vocabulary we use to describe political arguments. This language suggests that Woolf has written a piece of light, unprepossessing entertainment rather than a deeply felt critique of social and literary values.

In these reviews Woolf is the victim of the kind of condescension toward women writers that she describes in *A Room of One's Own*. These descriptions are not gender-neutral—it is hard to imagine a review calling a man's book "demure"—and they emphasize the stereotypical feminine quality of charm over masculine argument and logic. Even Woolf's wide-ranging knowledge of literary history must be domesticated as "decoration." The extreme version of these left-handed compliments, which heap adjectives on the essay's form and evade its content, appears in the *New York World*: praising Woolf's "smoothly-flowing prose," the critic gushes, "what matters her argument provided she keeps on writing books like this?"[10] Woolf here is the charming society hostess, chatting airily away without saying anything important.

When critics did explore her ideas, they were divided on their validity and originality. Some reviews argued that women had achieved equality as authors and that Woolf's argument was rather belated and irrelevant (*New York World*, 15). Others claimed that women were still at a disadvantage and that Woolf's sociological view of literary production, which took into account the circumstances of the writer's life and social milieu, represented a radical reinterpretation (*Herald-Tribune*, 1). Most of them wrestled with the question of whether or not Woolf was a feminist—a word that never appears in the essay but one that clearly characterizes many of its assumptions and conclusions. These attempts were complicated then, as they are today, by the question of what "feminism" means. If "feminist" means treating women as people rather than sex objects, then Woolf certainly is one, argued one reviewer.[11] At the other extreme, several reviews praised Woolf for not being a feminist and for providing, in the words of one critic, "an antidote to certain nonsensical ideas, quite widely entertained, about the ultimate elimination of the masculine principle in the world"—ideas that the reviewer regarded as the essence of feminism (*Criterion*, 511).

Many of the reviews selectively highlight the more moderate, less political passages in Woolf's argument, such as her warning against sex-consciousness, because they are less threatening and more acceptable. The influential *Times Literary Supplement* goes so far as to eliminate gender altogether as a primary concern of the essay. After surveying many of Woolf's arguments about women and writing, the reviewer concludes, "And her essay, while it glances in a spirited and good-tempered way over conflicts old and new, is really always bent on more intrinsic matters. These, one might say, are a love of life, a love of freedom and of letters; meeting in the conviction that if a writer does what he should he will bring us into the presence of reality" (867). Thus the reviewer redefines the real subject of Woolf's essay as "a love of life," and so forth—abstractions that are not entirely absent but seem remote from much of the argument—and claims that these matters are "more intrinsic" (the reviewer does not specify to what or to whom) than the essay's concentration on gender. Although far more flattering and high-flown than Arnold Bennett's misreading, this review also transforms Woolf's essay into something easier to digest—in this case a series of humanistic abstractions (I am tempted to say "platitudes") that efface the essay's political content.

Perhaps because they owe as much to fiction as to the essay tradition, Woolf's narrative strategies were also generally misread or ignored. The review that emphasizes the essay's demure tone is especially interesting given its claim that women often subdue their voices to please male critics. The author of this piece—in fact a woman—seems to have missed this essential point in Woolf's argument, along with Woolf's ironic manipulation of her narrator's tone to both enact and challenge injunctions against female self-assertion. The *New York Times Book Review* assumes that Woolf uses a persona to give "artificial personality to her remarks" rather than to dramatize the conflicts of the woman writer (2). In an early piece one critic calls attention to Woolf's use of the technique of interruption, using as an example the shift from a flight of poetry to the presentation of the soup at Oxbridge. The critic does not see that this shift is the point; material reality always intrudes in this essay to claim our attention and correct the tendency to ignore political and economic issues in discussions of art. Instead, the critic treats the interruption as an apolitical matter: "Whether it stems from the proclivity of the artist to examine the back as well as the front of the picture; or whether it is because of the intense fragility of poetic thought, the poet's need for relief after intense poetic concentration" (Lorberg, 151). She continues, "Such deviations at the expense of an idea are not permissible in serious writing" (Lorberg, 152).

Thus it is clear that Woolf's essay provoked a certain amount of confusion and discomfort among professional readers. In both technique and content, it clashed with presuppositions about Woolf's concerns as a writer, about gender and feminism, and about the essay form itself. *A Room of One's Own* was quickly subsumed into Woolf's writing as a work of secondary interest, something of a curiosity that was not directly related to her more important projects as an experimental writer of fiction and a bellelettristic literary critic.

Woolf's reputation declined somewhat in the 1930s. Facing the rise of fascism, a younger generation of writers and intellectuals found Woolf's emphasis on inner life and experimental technique evasive, even irresponsible. Moreover, she insisted on remaining a pacifist, as she and most of the Bloomsbury Group had been during World War I, despite her loathing for Hitler (both Woolf and her husband, a Jew, were on Hitler's death list). In an appreciative retrospective essay on Woolf, Angus Wilson remembers that "Mrs. Woolf was very low in my estimation then."[12] For younger writers, she was supplanted by the poets W. H. Auden, Christopher Isherwood, and Stephen Spender, who were outspoken and militant in their opposition to fascism. Woolf retained a considerable audience—her novel *The Years* (1937) was a best-seller in the United States, and she continued to be regarded as a major writer in England—but she was increasingly perceived as part of an older set of values that were becoming obsolete. After World War II a backlash against the privilege of the Bloomsbury set further eroded Woolf's reputation in England, while in the United States T. S. Eliot and James Joyce took their places as the preeminent modernist writers. Woolf's technical experiments and her complex use of language continue to interest critics in the United States, but, if she was not exactly perceived as second-rate, she has not always shared the critical limelight equally with these authors.

As interest in feminism died down in the 1930s, 1940s, and 1950s, *A Room of One's Own* took an increasingly marginal place in the Woolf canon. Once the vote was won, once women gained access to the universities, issues of gender seemed less pressing. Reflecting on Woolf's career after her death, E. M. Forster said, "In my judgment there is something old-fashioned about this extreme feminism; it dates back to her suffragette youth of the 1910's, when men kissed girls to distract them from wanting the vote, and very properly provoked her wrath."[13] In the same essay Forster refers to the "spots" of feminism "all over her work" (255). Forster's comment identifies feminism as a kind of a blemish and implies that it stands apart from her main concerns. For Forster, these political pock marks mar the smooth, beautiful surface of Woolf's prose, interrupting and distracting us from her more legitimate aesthetic aims. Forster's rigid separation of ideology and literature held sway for decades after Woolf's death, marginalizing her explicitly feminist essays, including *A Room of One's Own*, and effacing the explorations of gender and power that weave throughout much of her fiction and nonfiction.

The emergence of feminist criticism of the 1970s transformed people's understanding of Woolf's work, redefining her as a writer whose novels and essays are infused with concerns about the social world, particularly gender. While feminists were not the only critics to rediscover Woolf and write about her today, feminism has become the most visible critical approach to her works. By the late 1970s Woolf was one of the most written-about authors in the United States. Among modern feminists, as among Woolf's contemporaries, the essay has proved controversial. Because of Woolf's extraordinary resonance as a person and a symbol, in addition to the power of her writing, she has been the subject of what Brenda Silver has called "custody battles" over what brand of feminism she espouses and how progressive her ideas are.[14]

For critics who seek role models and ideological truths, *A Room of One's Own* succeeds or fails insofar as it offers a persuasive and inspirational critique of patriarchy. Some of these critics have praised *A Room of One's Own* for its compelling portrait of female authorship and have adapted it to their own studies of women writers and female literary history. *A Room of One's Own* has been praised, in both simple and sophisticated ways, for its radical insights into patriarchy, capitalism, literary and political modes of resistance, female psychology, female and lesbian sexuality. The title of an early article in this vein, "Storming the Toolshed," suggests the nature of this enterprise: assumed to reveal a coherent, although changing feminism, Woolf's writing provides the tools for analyzing and undoing the oppression of women.[15] According to this approach, the essay's content and narrative strategies offer models for new ways of thinking that remain relevant today. Thus *A Room of One's Own* is valued for its authentic insights, and Woolf emerges as a courageous feminist whose work empowers the women who come after her—much the same value that Woolf ascribes to a literary tradition in the essay itself.

Other critics, most famously Elaine Showalter and Adrienne Rich in the late 1970s, have complained that the elaborate narrative apparatus and "strenuous charm" of *A Room of One's Own* deliberately evade confrontation.[16] Rather than inspire women, the essay perpetuates inhibitions against female self-expression, particularly against female anger. In this view Woolf is guilty of maintaining a ladylike image in order to please men and protect herself when she should have expressed herself more directly and forcefully. More recently, Woolf has been criticized for her unconscious acceptance of her class privilege and the power relations of the British Empire (in her symbolic use of Africans and Turks, for example), despite her deliberate attempts to critique class structure and imperialism.

Still other critics, associated with poststructuralist schools of thought such as deconstruction and French feminism, praise *A Room of One's Own* and Woolf's work in general for the refusal to stake out a claim to a single truth. From this point of view Woolf's strength and value reside in her obstinate questioning (to borrow a phrase from Wordsworth) and rejection of definitive insights, whether in the form of the perorations she rejects explicitly in *A Room of One's Own* or of a particular conclusion about the nature of women. The title of a recent work of criticism, *Virginia Woolf: Feminist Destinations*, captures this sense of open-endedness; it implies a train of thought that is first of all in motion and second of all not limited to a single endpoint.[17]

It is certainly a tribute to the complexity of the issues that *A Room of One's Own* raises that it should be regarded in so many different lights. Its multifaceted reception has been influenced by its own complex narrative strategies and by the rapidly-changing nature of feminist literary criticism. Fittingly, it is unlikely that there will ever be a party line on *A Room of One's Own*. Instead, it seems destined to continually reopen conversations about freedom and power, politics and art, women and men.

4

Women's Colleges and *A Room of One's Own*

In October 1928 Virginia Woolf traveled to Cambridge University to deliver two talks. She was invited by the Arts Society of Newnham College and the Odtaa at Girton College, then the only women's colleges at Cambridge. Unable to enroll in the university as a student, Woolf entered it as an adult, and a woman, on her own terms. While in 1932 she declined an invitation from Cambridge University to deliver the prestigious Clark Lectures in English literature, which had been inaugurated by her own father, she quickly accepted the women students' offer five years earlier. She saw her visit as part of a continuing struggle for women's empowerment: "I wanted to encourage young women," she wrote to a friend, "they seem to get fearfully depressed" (*Letters*, 4: 106).

These talks grew into the book we know as *A Room of One's Own* as well as the essay "Women and Fiction," which first appeared in the journal the *Forum* in 1929. Although the general arguments remained the same, Woolf made significant changes as she revised her presentations for publication: for example, the section on Judith Shakespeare, probably the most famous part of the essay today, did not appear in the original talks. According to the editor of Woolf's manuscript, it seems clear that "the experience itself of coming to Cambridge and reading a paper to a women's college on women and fiction became the narrative basis for the book."[1] The well-known contrast between the meals at Oxbridge and Fernham, the fictional men's and women's universities of *A Room of One's Own*, grew from Woolf's visit to the university, where she did dine at both a men's and a women's college (although, according to one eyewitness, she visited the women's college first, and the men's college served only one kind of wine rather than the two described in her fictional account) (Rosenbaum, xv–xvi).

Along with Woolf's concrete experiences, an intensified sense of the meaning of the women's colleges probably shaped the final essay. Certainly they were an appropriate setting for Woolf's reflections on women's roles, for their history embodied many of the same issues Woolf raised in *A Room of One's Own*. Their lurching progress toward equality reflected the male-dominated culture that Woolf set out to analyze. Along with Oxford, Cambridge was a bastion of male privilege well into the twentieth century—indeed, until almost 20 years after her talk women were not admitted to full membership at Cambridge despite the fact that they had attended lectures there since the late nineteenth century. When Emily Davies founded Girton in 1869 and Anne Jemima Clough founded Newnham in 1871, the first women's colleges to take their place alongside the male colleges at Cambridge, some of which dated from the Middle Ages. They were not established without a fight, nor did their founding end discrimination. The women's dormitories were situated a safe distance from the existing university to minimize the distraction to male students; women were allowed only to attend lectures, where seating was segregated by sex, but not to take degrees. Like Woolf's anonymous narrator, the teachers at the women's colleges had only limited access to the Cambridge library.[2] (Even 100 years later such conflicts continue: in the summer of 1993, during the writing of this book, women dons at Oxford were battling for the promotion of more women, who accounted for only 4 percent of the faculty.)

Despite these frustrations, college was a heady experience for young women accustomed to the tedium of middle-class ladyhood. They arrived there, one student said,

> Sick to the soul, you know, my friend,
> Of balls and croquet without end
> An empty life and ne'er an aim
> Worth spending strength on.[3]

At college they found many of the prerequisites to achievement enumerated in *A Room of One's Own*. College provided a sustaining community and an independent existence rather than the contingent identity of "the squire's daughter, or the clergyman's, or the doctor's" (Williams, 180) to which they were accustomed. It also encouraged them to reject the damaging strictures against women's self-expression that have left women, in the words of *A Room of One's Own*, "so terribly accustomed to concealment and suppression" (84). This theme of silence and self-expression runs throughout Woolf's thinking. In her famous essay "Professions for Women" she wages war against the stereotypical Victorian woman, the Angel in the House, who advises the budding writer, "My dear, you are a young woman. . . . Never let anybody guess that you have a mind of your own."[4] We remember her half-brother's comment, "They're not used to women saying *anything*."

The women's community at Cambridge, however, challenged that conventional social training. It encouraged women to express themselves without muting their intelligence or their passion. Reporting her triumph at a college debate, one student wrote, "I really was intensely interested in my subject, and I did so want some of them to agree with me, and the result was that I spoke for some minutes without the slightest hesitation or difficulty, and, a thing I have never done before, spoke of my own feelings on the subject—I mean, what I really feel, not what I feel when I am asked my opinion" (quoted in Williams, 180). Freed of social and family obligations, freed of the need to defer to men, these women could experiment with different roles and voices, like Woolf's imaginary novelist Mary Carmichael, who can assert that "Chloe liked Olivia" once she is certain that no men are present. Indeed, in the single-sex world of the women's college, women are free to act out the subversive message of that imaginary novelist and like each other.

Most striking in light of Woolf's essay, college women found an autonomous space. They had privacy in which to study, talk, and dream without the distractions of the common sitting room—that private/public space where, Woolf argues, women are always on call to perform their domestic role. No family and friends interrupted their work with requests to darn socks or pay afternoon calls; no intruder questioned the value of the work they had chosen. Emily Davies called this "perhaps the most distinctive feature of college life"—"this great boon—the power of being alone" (quoted in Williams, 181). Woolf, of course, called it a room of one's own.

A READING

5

Women and Society: Patriarchy and the Place of the Outsider

Masterpieces are not single and solitary births; they are the outcomes of many years of thinking in common. (65)

In a sense, it is an exercise in irony to write about *A Room of One's Own* as a "masterwork," since Woolf's essay argues forcefully against the traditional notion of a masterpiece as the spontaneous and timeless creation of an individual genius. Masterpieces are not created in isolation, without context or history. Instead, Woolf claims, they are the culmination of a tradition, and they can only flower in a material environment that supports—or at least does not impede—the artist. Women, living in a male world, lack the necessary autonomy to create freely. Hence Woolf's famous prescription: a woman needs a room of her own and £500 a year.[1] Exploring the constraints on women's achievement, *A Room of One's Own* analyzes the hostile environment in which women write and the responses, both creative and self-defeating, that this environment provokes.

A *Room of One's Own* turns on two large, vague words: patriarchy and feminism. "Patriarchy" refers to the male world that women
occupy uneasily. "The most transient visitor to this planet, I thought,
who picked up this [news]paper could not fail to be aware, even from
this scattered testimony, that England is under the rule of patriarchy,"
the narrator claims (33). Patriarchy has historically been defined as a
society that passes down property and family identity through the male
line, from father to son (thus the tradition of a women taking on her
father's name at birth and her husband's when she marries). Woolf
uses the term more loosely, describing a social organization in which
men monopolize power in its socially recognized forms, including but
not limited to economic power. Thus the men in the narrator's news-
paper are gold magnates in South Africa (though gender is not mentioned, the narrator's comments indicate that the "somebody" is male),
diplomats, and judges; the only woman mentioned is an actress who is
suspended in midair in—where else?—California, apparently acting as
a prop for a publicity stunt of someone else's devising and for someone
else's benefit.

In addition to presenting patriarchy as a social system, Woolf
also regards patriarchy as an *ideology*, a system of beliefs and values
that naturalizes itself—that is, that makes its assumptions look like the
result of common sense and some universal human nature rather than
of vested political interests. Ideology is a powerful means of sustaining
the status quo: it is easier and more effective to persuade people that
the current distribution of power is natural and inevitable than to protect it with coercion or force. So men not only monopolize power, but
they do so on the basis of some alleged natural right or capacity that
women are said to lack.

Woolf confronted this attitude in many places. As a form of
social organization, patriarchy was written into law. She reminds us in
A Room of One's Own that no women in England could vote until
1918. Until 1870—only 12 years before Woolf was born—a married
woman did not have the right to retain either her own wages or inherited property; all of her material possessions belonged to her husband.
And although women gained access to higher education in the nineteenth century, they could not graduate from colleges in Oxford or

Cambridge until the early 1920s. As an ideology, patriarchy permeated beliefs about appropriate female activities. Woolf confronted these beliefs within her family: her beloved brother Thoby went cheerfully off to Cambridge while she stayed home to be educated by her parents and private tutors. Although her education was rigorous and extensive, she did not miss the message of male privilege. Writing to Thoby about Shakespeare's *Cymbeline* when she is 19, she says, "I shall want a lecture when I see you; to clear up some points about the Plays. . . . Imogen and Posthumous and Cymbeline—I find them beyond me—Is this my feminine weakness in the upper region?"[2] The young Woolf has internalized patriarchal ideology, assuming that her gender enfeebles her reading of Shakespeare.

As the Oxbridge section of *A Room of One's Own* suggests, Woolf did not forget her early feelings of exclusion and inferiority, so poignantly expressed here in her desire for a lecture. Indeed, British society did not let her forget them. Despite her literary fame, she continued to face the prejudices of patriarchal ideology. In 1935 her friend E. M. Forster told her that the London Library Committee had refused to invite her membership because, according to her father (once a member of the committee, now dead for 30 years), women were "so troublesome."[3] Like the narrator in *A Room of One's Own*, she found herself shut out of a significant cultural institution. At the time of her rejection, she had published eight novels, including *Mrs. Dalloway, To the Lighthouse*, and *The Waves*, along with several volumes of essays and short stories, and was widely considered one of the major literary talents of the period. With her husband, she also ran the Hogarth Press, which published some of the most significant literature of the time. Perhaps even more than the committee's rejection, the attitude of her friend Forster, a member of the committee, galled her: Forster (who had not published a novel in over a decade) reported the decision casually, as if it were an amusing anecdote, and made no attempt to contest the committee's decision, except to ask rather lamely if ladies might not have improved since Leslie Stephen's day.

Woolf encountered aspects of this ideology in the most important opinion-making journals of her age as well. One might think that what the Victorians called "The Woman Question" might have been laid to rest with the passage of ameliorative legislation throughout the nineteenth and early twentieth century. Although suffrage and full educational enfranchisement were gained only in 1928, when Woolf wrote *A Room of One's Own*, women had much the same legal status as men. But the issue of women's abilities continued to be debated. In particular, the writings of Desmond MacCarthy stimulated Woolf to argument and resistance. Their exchange provides an important, immediate context to the arguments of *A Room of One's Own*. It quite possibly supplied the initial impetus for the project, and certainly it suggests the extent and nature of patriarchal thinking in British society. It is worth looking at the exchange in some detail.

In 1920 MacCarthy gave a favorable review in the *New Statesman* to a book by the novelist Arnold Bennett entitled *Our Women*, which concluded that women were naturally inferior to men and in fact wished to be dominated by them. MacCarthy's endorsement of this view offended Woolf in several ways. For one thing, MacCarthy was a personal friend whom Woolf knew as a classmate of her brother Thoby at Cambridge along with the other men of the Bloomsbury Group. Like Forster, he failed to find friendship with and respect for Woolf incompatible with sexism. One can only imagine Woolf's frustration at being surrounded by these intellectual male friends who could proclaim the inferiority of women. Did she belong or didn't she? Additionally, the *New Statesman* was one of the most prestigious intellectual papers of the time; Woolf herself wrote for it in the late 1930s, and her husband was asked to be its literary editor—the job MacCarthy held—when it merged with the *Nation* in 1930. MacCarthy's support of Bennett's views, then, was highly visible, highly credible, and close to home. Moreover, Bennett himself was a writer whom Woolf did not completely respect. A few years later she criticized his style of writing in the now-famous essay "Mr. Bennett and Mrs. Brown," comparing it unfavorably with the modernist experiments that she and other writers were practicing. Feeling herself to be Bennett's artistic and intellectual superior, Woolf was doubly annoyed at his wholesale denigration of women.

Women and Society: Patriarchy and the Place of the Outsider

Her response to MacCarthy and Bennett, also published in the *New Statesman*, outlines many of her arguments in *A Room of One's Own*. Woolf regards what she considers the improvement of women's writing from the Duchess of Newcastle to Jane Austen and concludes that "the effects of education and liberty [are] scarcely to be overrated."[4] In other words, in contrast to the patriarchal assertion of natural and innate incapacity, women's achievements are largely determined by their training and opportunities. Woolf lays out the conditions which would nurture women's achievement: women should be able to "think, invent, imagine, and create as freely as men do, and with as little fear of ridicule and condescension" (*Diary*, 2: 342). And, she continues, men such as Bennett and MacCarthy constitute active impediments to women's achievement, not because they pass laws forbidding women to write but because they perpetuate patriarchal ideology in their writing. How could a young woman nourish her desire to write after reading that one of England's most famous novelists believed in her innate and insurmountable incapacity? Woolf also asserts the importance of tradition, the "many years of thinking in common" (65). She states, "You will not get a big [Sir Isaac] Newton until you have produced a considerable number of lesser Newtons" (*Diary*, 2: 341).

Even more galling was MacCarthy's assessment of Woolf's own achievement, which appeared in print only a few months before Woolf delivered her lectures at Newnham and Girton. In *Life and Letters* MacCarthy claims that "female novelists should only aspire to excellence by courageously acknowledging the limitations of their sex (Jane Austen and, in our time, Mrs. Virginia Woolf have demonstrated how gracefully this gesture can be accomplished)" (75n). MacCarthy's glib assertions that women have innate limitations as writers and that they ought to embrace their inferiority—along with the condescending praise of this internalization as a graceful gesture, something like pouring out tea in the drawing room—are classic patriarchal assumptions. It is easy to imagine how angry such a left-handed compliment would have made Woolf, even though it places her in the company of her beloved Jane Austen.

Woolf quotes this passage in *A Room of One's Own*, but, significantly, she leaves out the reference to herself (75). Is she attempting to avoid having her arguments dismissed as mere personal grievance—that damaging attitude for which she chastises women writers such as Charlotte Brontë? In this passage the gap is significant—and the significance of gaps, blank spaces, and absences is a subject to which we will return, for it is central to the construction of the essay. Here, it signals the difficulties of Woolf's position as both a woman writer and a feminist literary critic: on the one hand, she must argue against the assumptions of patriarchy, but on the other, since those assumptions are directed against her and since they make her angry, she is vulnerable to charges of personal pique, which might compromise her objectivity. For Woolf, at this point the simplest strategy was to omit direct personal reference, which would certainly have raised the eyebrows of her readers. For the women writers in *A Room of One's Own*, including the narrator Mary Beton, this double bind remains a central, disabling problem. Thus patriarchal assumptions directly impinged on Woolf as a writer, and *A Room of One's Own* reflects the lines of thinking she developed in opposition to these assumptions.

In thinking through the problem of patriarchy, Woolf evolved a politics that insisted on several points: the importance of gender as a category in society, the fact of women's oppression, and the extent of women's abilities and values when left untrammeled by male domination. This brings us to the second key word in Woolf's argument: feminism. Although it is never mentioned, it is routinely applied to Woolf's essay. Interestingly, Woolf herself appears to reject the word in her essay *Three Guineas*, calling it "a dead word, a corrupt word. Let us therefore celebrate this occasion by cremating the corpse."[5] But, as usual, there is considerable playfulness and irony in this hyperbolic assertion. Woolf rejects "feminism" because she says the only important right of women—the right to earn a living—has already been won. But she goes on to celebrate the fight for equality and justice for all people. The essence of *Three Guineas* is to explain the interlocking patriarchal oppressions of sexism, imperialism, and class struggle. Woolf does not so much abandon the cause of women as join it with related causes.

Certainly Woolf's writing reveals a lifelong interest in women's writing and in the status of women: along with her long essays *A Room of One's Own* and *Three Guineas*, she has also written several shorter essays, including the well-known "Women and Fiction," the outgrowth of *A Room of One's Own*, and "Professions for Women," as well as a large number of discussions of individual women writers. Readers of *A Room of One's Own* can turn to Woolf's collected essays for fuller treatments of Jane Austen, Charlotte and Emily Brontë, Christina Rossetti, George Eliot, the Duchess of Newcastle, Aphra Behn, and Dorothy Osborne, as well as such wide-ranging literary figures as Katherine Mansfield, Dorothy Richardson, Mme de Sévigné, Mary Wollstonecraft, Sara Coleridge, Elizabeth Gaskell, Mrs. Humphrey Ward, and Olive Schreiner. As this list suggests, Woolf did not confine her interests to canonical writers; she continued her project beyond *A Room of One's Own*, acknowledging and reevaluating women who were obscure as well as famous and who wrote in many genres, including letters and diaries.

But the question remains: What sort of feminist was Woolf? The question is difficult to answer, at least in part because Woolf resisted definitive labels and allegiances. Throughout her career Woolf addressed issues that we now consider feminist. Although she does not hew to any party line, certain ideas and concerns recur in her writing about women. She treats them with complexity and sometimes with ambivalence; her feminism is more a sustained commitment to thinking about women's issues than a matter of a simple dogma.

Certainly Woolf was what is called a social or cultural feminist: she was especially interested in how woman's particular social place gave rise to distinctively female values and sensibilities. The term "social feminist" is generally distinguished from "political feminist," which refers to someone who argues for women's empowerment on the basis of their identity with men. Woolf clearly believed that women were men's equals, but she also consistently privileged women's *difference* from men in her fiction and nonfiction. For example, Woolf grants a surprising importance to Clarissa Dalloway's party-giving in *Mrs. Dalloway*, which becomes a kind of life-affirming ritual and a sustaining force for human relationships. Here, as in *To the Lighthouse*, through the figure of the maternal Mrs. Ramsay (also an expert party-giver), Woolf paints a vivid picture of a distinctive woman's culture. Yet at the same time she retains an ambivalence about such traditional forms of femininity. We remember her scathing portrait of the Angel in the House in "Professions for Women"—the Victorian ideal of decorative, subservient womanhood: "Directly, that is to say, I took my pen in hand to review that novel by a famous man, she slipped behind me and whispered: 'My dear, you are a young woman. You are writing about a book that has been written by a man. Be sympathetic; be tender; flatter; deceive; use all the arts and wiles of our sex. Never let anybody guess that you have a mind of your own'" ("Professions," 237). Woolf turns to the Angel and strangles her, saying, "Had I not killed her she would have killed me. She would have plucked the heart out of my writing" (238). Woolf's double attitude toward traditional femininity makes itself felt in *A Room of One's Own*.

While Woolf's recurring emphasis on the difference between women and men might seem to essentialize gender—that is, to suggest that there are unchanging and inherent characteristics that mark men and women—at several points she takes pains to insist that these differences are socially constructed and therefore subject to change. In fact, much of *A Room of One's Own* is devoted to tracing the effect of social restrictions on female personality. Although it is sometimes muted, the process of historical change can be felt in her novels and essays as a force that can transform consciousness. Woolf's celebrated assertion in "Mr. Bennett and Mrs. Brown"—that "on or about December, 1910, human character changed"—is a whimsical version of her belief in the historically specific nature of identity.[6]

A Room of One's Own predicts an era when women will become soldiers and dock laborers and will presumably lose their shyness and reticence in the process. Because Woolf characteristically associates war and violence with men—most notably in *Mrs. Dalloway* and *Three Guineas*—the suggestion that women will become soldiers has the potential to radically alter both women's gender identity and the relationship of that identity to masculinity. In much, although by no means all, of her work, Woolf follows traditional thought by portraying men and women as polar opposites: women nurture feelings, men think abstractly; women are self-effacing, men are self-assertive. Women's engagement in aggressive activities would undo this opposition, disrupting the structure of gender as we know it. Already, Woolf finds, historical events have changed the emotions between men and women: having exposed male leaders as "ugly" and "stupid," Woolf claims, World War I has rendered impossible the romantic sentiments of the poets Tennyson and Christina Rossetti (15).

Woolf entered a new territory when she attempted to write about women in an overtly political way. She was an experimental novelist, not a philosopher or a political scientist, and she had to find her own forms of expression. Her interest in the concrete historical and social context of gender roles was, until the 1930s, allusive and sporadic rather than sustained and detailed. *A Room of One's Own* represents a turning point in her public presentation of feminism: while drawing heavily on the techniques of fiction, it also argues an ideological point about the status of women. Woolf experiments with a few footnotes, but the essay does not attempt to follow the form of a tightly structured logical argument. As Woolf grew older, she tried more and more to make use of the kind of arguments and evidence that might prove a case without abandoning her interest in formal experiments. In some ways her feminist writing presents her with the same challenge as her novels: to meld the "granite-like solidity" of the real world with the "rainbow-like intangibility" of insight and imagination.[7]

In the novel *The Years* (1937) and the essay *Three Guineas* (1938) Woolf works harder to introduce the granite of fact into her feminist prose and so to draw a more detailed picture of the relationship between social reality and human consciousness, especially as that relationship shapes gender identity. In *The Years*, which she originally called a novel-essay, she intended to interpolate fictional chapters about a family named Pargiter from 1880 to "the present day" with factual chapters detailing the legal, social, and economic status of women in the relevant historical period. Conceived as a sequel to *A Room of One's Own*, this ambitious work eventually split itself into the novel *The Years* and the essays "Professions for Women" and *Three Guineas*, the latter a heavily footnoted, although still fictionalized, analysis of patriarchal oppression. Thus, placing *A Room of One's Own* in the context of Woolf's career, we might say that it reflects the more impressionistic portraits of femininity from the novels of the 1920s and also looks ahead to the more analytical and historical approach to women's status that characterized some of her writing in the 1930s. While Woolf's understanding of femininity and her interest in social context remained constant, she shifted her emphasis and presentation in her continuing engagement with feminism.

Woolf's central approach to this project places *A Room of One's Own* squarely at the center of the feminist strategy that the contemporary poet Adrienne Rich outlines in her essay "When We Dead Awaken: Writing as Re-Vision." For Rich, "re-vision" is more than simply tinkering with an existing social reality, as we might use the word when we speak of revising an essay. She means a much more radical undoing of assumptions—to see the world anew and to imagine as-yet unrealized possibilities, as her hyphenation suggests in its emphasis on the word "vision." Rich explains,

> A radical critique of literature, feminist in its impulse, would take the work first of all as a clue to how we live, how we have been living, how we have been led to imagine ourselves, how our language has trapped as well as liberated us; and how we can begin to see—and therefore live—afresh. A change in the concept of sexual identity is essential is we are not going to see the old political order re-assert itself in every new revolution. We need to know the writing of the past, and know it differently than we have ever known it; not to pass on a tradition but to break its hold over us.[8]

Like Rich, Woolf attempts to reevaluate conventional truths about men and women, about the value of tradition, about the status of man-made facts and history. She wants to make visible the ideology of patriarchy, which cloaks itself in the notions of common sense and human nature, in order to undo its mystifications and break its hold over us, as Rich says. Woolf seeks to find a different history and tell a different story to bring women's experience into clearer focus.

I want to look at a few moments of re-vision to suggest Woolf's approach to her material. A simple example would be her assertion that "if I were rewriting history, I should describe more fully and think of greater importance than the Crusades or the War of the Roses . . . [the fact that the] middle-class woman began to write" (65). This example questions the notion of history as objective and universal. It challenges conventional definitions of history as a record of battles and governments, turning instead to what we might call social history—that is, what ordinary people did in their everyday lives, apart from public politics—and to women's history—now a full-blown academic field that Woolf anticipates in this brief passage. Only men fought in the Crusades and the War of the Roses; what were women doing? We might ask not only what history is about but whom it is for. If we take women as an important audience for history, then the fact that middle-class women began to write in the nineteenth century might well be considered more important than the Crusades, in which women did not participate.

We might also look at her use of Arthur Quiller-Couch's discussion of class and authorship among male writers. Quiller-Couch makes essentially the same argument as Woolf: that the material circumstances of would-be writers, including their educational opportunities, have an enormous effect on their achievements. Woolf uses Quiller-Couch's argument as support for her own claims, but she also revises his argument by introducing women authors. In doing so she makes visible their absence in Quiller-Couch's original claims—much as the narrator's trespass reveals the exclusion of women at Oxbridge. Despite his sensitivity to class and economic issues, Quiller-Couch does not even consider women writers in his theory, although, as *A Room of One's Own* suggests, women such as Austen, the Brontës, and George Eliot were prominent contemporaries of the male writers Quiller-Couch discusses. Woolf's re-visioning, then, sees women where they were absent before.

Elsewhere in the essay, Woolf writes of the "blank spaces" on library bookshelves where women's books should be, seeing not mere accidental absence but exclusion (52). It is the "books that were not there" that tell the tale of women's literary history (45). Woolf implies here a politics of absence, continuing the spatial imagery of her title as well as the imagery of vision, by defining these empty spaces as having been created by gender inequities. Although there is nothing there, that "nothing" still has meaning, just as rests have meaning in a system of musical notation. This is another version of re-vision: to see blank space as its own kind of historical record, just as she sees potential artists in madwomen and witches (49).

The process of re-vision reveals the blind spot in Quiller-Couch's very useful theory—perhaps a blind spot the size of a shilling, as the narrator metaphorically calls men's ignorance about women (90). Woolf does not suggest that Quiller-Couch deliberately excludes women from his theory. He simply did not think of including them and did not notice their omission because, at the time when he was writing, the question of their exclusion was not in the air as it was when Woolf was writing. As Adrienne Rich says in her essay, "Until we can understand the assumptions in which we are drenched" we cannot see things in new ways (Rich, 176). Quiller-Couch's exclusion of women is neither an accident nor an act of deliberate prejudice; it is a good example of the workings of ideology, which drenches us in its assumptions to the point where we cannot see our prejudices—we understand them, as I have said, as natural. If women are assumed to be intellectually and artistically inferior to men, then they will not be included in theories about art, however progressive those theories might be in other ways.

Perhaps the most interesting moments of re-vision turn on metaphors of vision itself. Two examples present themselves. The first involves Woolf's idea of women as mirrors that present a flattering image of men to themselves. For Woolf, this relationship between men and women is one of the crucial props of traditional masculinity; it is the basis of the ideology of male superiority. If women dismantle it by refusing to act as mirrors, men will change as well as women: "How is he to go on giving judgment, civilising natives, making laws, writing books, dressing up and speechifying at banquets, unless he can see himself at breakfast and dinner at least twice the size he really is?" (36). The answer to this rhetorical question is, of course, "He can't." What, then, would men do? What would they be like? Woolf does not attempt to answer this question, but clearly when men see themselves differently, they will behave differently.

Another passage suggests, with a vengeance, what mirror-women might reflect if they decided to reflect a different image of masculinity. After the narrator has been chased by the beadle and excluded from the library, she passes the Oxbridge chapel and does not even attempt to enter it. She sees the congregation moving about inside, "like bees at the mouth of a hive," and describes it this way: "Many were in cap and gown; some had tufts of fur on their shoulders; others were wheeled in bath-chairs; others, though not past middle age, seemed creased and crushed into shapes so singular that one was reminded of those giant crabs and crayfish who heave with difficulty across the sand of an aquarium" (8). This grotesque vision of male academics appealed to Woolf; she repeats it, in altered form, in *Jacob's Room*, where Cambridge men attending chapel service look like insects flying blindly around a lantern. Once again male oppression influences this portrait: "Why allow women to take part in it?" asks Jacob, the Cambridge student, after the narrator (explicitly female in the novel) has described it.[9]

Being excluded creates a particular point of view for these narrators. They literally gaze at the spectacle from the outside, peering through windows; metaphorically they are outsiders in a deeper sense because they cannot claim full citizenship in this cultural world. Woolf describes the dislocation of women in their own society: "If one is a woman one is often surprised by a sudden splitting off of consciousness, say, walking down Whitehall, when from being the natural inheritor of that civilisation, she becomes, on the contrary, outside of it, alien and critical" (97). From the outside Woolf's narrators re-vision the imputed ceremonial dignity of the service as a bizarre, mindless ritual because they are not part of it. Their perspective mixes anger, resentment, irreverence, and a kind of productive ignorance: having not been fully assimilated into this world, perhaps not knowing the meaning of all its academic regalia (the "tufts of fur on their shoulders") and formulaic behaviors, these women see it with fresh eyes, like the child who calls out, "The Emperor has no clothes." Clearly their personal irritation at being excluded has something to do with the transformation of Cambridge dons into crabs and insects, but it is equally true that Woolf also intends a more telling critique of what she considers to be the empty and self-aggrandizing pomposity of academic rituals.

This point emerges directly at the end of *A Room of One's Own*, when she jokes about the pointlessness of receiving a "highly ornamental pot" from a headmaster (106). It also animates much of *Three Guineas*, in which the extended first chapter critiques academic hierarchies as nurturing the will to power that also motivates war. In these passages we see that, while women's marginality disenfranchises them from important forms of cultural power, it also gives them a critical perspective, a new angle of vision, on their society. They lack the privilege that makes the apparent naturalness of patriarchy go unquestioned, and they are not as fully trained and assimilated into dominant values and institutions. In *Three Guineas* Woolf imagines a paradoxical "Outsiders' Society," populated by women, who can retain their integrity because they are not corrupted by male privilege (*Guineas*, 106). Ironically, the exclusion of women from Oxbridge because of their alleged inferiority puts them in a position from which to question male superiority. The importance of perspective or vantage point, implied in the metaphor of vision, becomes clear here. While also "drenched" in patriarchal ideology, the discomfort of their oppression leads women to rethink their world. This is the origin of Rich's re-vision—seeing from a different place.

Another way of understanding these moments is in terms of the metaphor of the title. The different place from which women speak is one of the "blank spaces" (52) that Woolf attempts to recover and redefine. Nowhere becomes somewhere; she imagines transforming the outsider's position, standing at the margins looking in, into the protected, autonomous space of one's own room. Against the weighty public spaces of Oxbridge and the British Museum, and against the claustrophobic public drawing room that imprisons traditional femininity, she posits a third, private space that escapes, to some degree, the precepts of patriarchal ideology. Woolf means this literally: she reminds us of how important such a sheltering space is to us—a place where we can feel that we are ourselves (however much of an illusion this feeling might be), temporarily free of social roles and expectations, mercifully protected from prying eyes and admonitions. The various "Keep Out" signs that children put on their doors suggest the importance of this boundary in maintaining a sense of control over one's environment, and even over one's identity; the door to one's room is one of those sacred barriers, like the cover of one's diary, that cannot be broached uninvited without violating some profound sense of self.

As this discussion of rooms suggests, Woolf also evokes the metaphorical sense of psychological privacy implied in the popular slogan, "I need my own space." The contrast between Jane Austen's sitting room and the imagined room of one's own implies the paradox of women in domestic space: the home is supposed to be their province, but, Woolf implies, they are never quite at home there. The private sphere of the home is also culturally constructed, not a magical place exempt from the values and demands of public space, as the Victorians claimed, but an extension of them in somewhat different form. Women are trapped in the sphere over which they preside—wielding considerable power, perhaps, over the practices of family life but unable to claim their autonomy or assert their needs within it. Jane Austen writes in between "all kinds of casual interruptions" (67) that intrude into the common sitting room, and Florence Nightingale complains, "Women never have a half an hour . . . that they can call their own" (66).

For Woolf, space is a political and economic construction as well as a physical and psychological one. All of the spaces in the essay are economically determined: we need only think of her description of Oxbridge, of the opulent dinner and the coffers of gold that pour into its construction, to see that those august buildings come into existence and maintain themselves because of very concrete forms of privilege and power. For Woolf, economic independence is the basis of psychological and intellectual independence because it frees women from the need to defer to men, to act as their aggrandizing mirror in exchange for material support. The room of one's own is both the sign that a woman writer has achieved economic independence and the means by which she can continue to do so, for it provides her with a protected space in which to write.

As the narrator of the essay, Woolf takes on the status of outsider to analyze patriarchy. She refers to herself as "one who has no training in a university" (28) and, quite disingenuously, an "uneducated Englishwoman" (108). Clearly Woolf can hardly be considered uneducated; her essay is peppered with names of authors and titles of books that many readers will not have read or perhaps even have heard of. In her discussion of teaching *A Room of One's Own*, Marcia McClintock Folsom cites this disingenuousness as a source of discomfort among her students, who ask, "'How can she claim to have been left out . . . when she obviously knows so much more than I do and writes so well?'"[10] Partly, perhaps, her claims of ignorance are strategic: look how much the uneducated Englishwoman knows, she might be saying, as a way of putting male education in its place. Given the portrait of male academics as insects and crayfish, it may be an honor to be uneducated.

Woolf clings to her outsider status as a form of integrity, and this impulse may underlie her overstatement of her lack of education. When Woolf declined the opportunity to give the prestigious Clark Lectures on English literature at Cambridge University in 1932, she remarked sardonically to a friend, "Isn't that a compliment for an illiterate (who cant spell) of my sex?"[11] Without understanding Woolf's attitudes about the advantages of exclusion and marginality, we can only find her refusal astonishing. The lectures are extremely prestigious, and she was the first woman invited to deliver them; her presence at Cambridge would seem to acknowledge the intellectual equality of women. They would provide her with a chance to appear in a position of honor at the place of her exclusion. Furthermore, past lectures had been delivered not only by her friend/enemy Desmond MacCarthy but also by her own father, who would not consider sending her to a university. The opportunity for personal revenge must have been tempting, but Woolf's explanation for refusing explains her reasons: "Think of me, the uneducated child reading books in my room at 22 H.P.G. [Hyde Park Gate, her childhood home]—now advanced to this glory. But I shall refuse, because how could I write 6 lectures, to be delivered in full term, without giving up a year to criticism; without becoming a functionary; without sealing my lips when it comes to tilting at Universities" (*Diary*, 4: 79).

Woolf wants to devote her time to fiction rather than criticism, but, more important, she does not wish to become part of the university, to implicitly grant it her approval, or to feel beholden or identified with it, which would inhibit her criticism. We sense that Woolf wishes to pay some kind of homage to the "uneducated" and "illiterate" child she once felt herself to be by not burying that lack of privilege in the prestige of the Cambridge lectures. In *Three Guineas* she styles herself more accurately as one of the "daughters of educated men," but in *A Room of One's Own* she emphasizes her disenfranchisement instead.

In light of these concerns, Woolf manages her position as speaker at the women's colleges, and later as narrator of the essay, very carefully. Patrick McGee says, "She enters the university and assumes the position of lecturer without surrendering for a moment her status as an outsider"[12] just as the women students in her audience are also outsiders, in some sense, although they have been allowed to occupy a space within the university. Moreover, her essay would certainly not be a model college lecture, authoritative and easily outlined. Woolf works hard, in fact, to avoid giving a lecture of the sort she so poignantly requested of her brother Thoby on *Cymbeline*, for that would undermine her integrity as an outsider.

Jane Marcus claims that in *A Room of One's Own* "Virginia Woolf deconstructs the lecture as a form"; she quotes Woolf as writing, "'Lecturing incites the most debased of human passions—vanity, ostentation, self-assertion, and the desire to convert.'"[13] Instead Woolf uses a circuitous, indirect narrative structure and slyly inserts some research topics for women students at university—the effects of psychology on the minds of artists (52–53), the history of men's opposition to the suffrage movement (55), and the importance of women's chastity to men (64), for instance. Woolf's lecture is not a self-contained, definitive pronouncement on her subject but a springboard for other women, providing opportunities for the development of a female intellectual tradition.

6

A Sociology of Creativity

What makes a writer—or a poet, a musician, a painter, or an artist of any sort? Is it primarily talent and hard work—will any artist with real talent find her calling and succeed? Few people would deny that luck and opportunity play a role, but Woolf goes much further in suggesting that the material conditions of a person's life will dramatically affect her ability to produce art and the kind of art she makes. Woolf says, "Fiction is like a spider's web, attached ever so lightly perhaps, but still attached to life at all four corners" (41). This relationship between creativity and what Woolf calls here "life"—and what appears elsewhere in *A Room of One's Own* as society, patriarchy, and Empire—is central to Woolf's argument. It shifts the grounds of the debate about women's achievement: the issue is no longer women's innate abilities but the social structures that inhibit or facilitate freedom of mind, as Woolf insists in her exchange with Desmond MacCarthy.

Regarding women's achievement alongside historical increases in education and liberty, Woolf observes, "The advance in intellectual power seems to me not only sensible but immense" (*Diary*, 2: 339).

Thus Woolf finds it impossible to address the question of why Elizabethan women did not write poetry until she can find out how they were educated, how many children they had, or whether they had a room of their own (46). In *A Room of One's Own* Woolf demystifies the relationship between art and the material world—that is, she strips off the illusion that art exists in some special, privileged cultural zone that exempts it from the considerations of money, politics, social class, and, especially, gender.

Opposed to Woolf's position is the idea that art is transcendent, rising above the particular conditions of its composition. These spatial metaphors imply a hierarchy: the material is inferior, the artistic superior; it is not only a characteristic of art but art's purpose to move beyond or above the real world. This idea, against which Woolf argues in *A Room of One's Own*, was forcefully expressed by her friend T. S. Eliot in a famous essay titled "Tradition and the Individual Talent" (1919). Although Woolf would certainly have agreed with much of Eliot's essay, especially his valorization of tradition, his emphasis on what he calls his "impersonal theory of poetry" denies the relevance of context, except for literary history, on a work of art.[1] Eliot wants to build an impenetrable wall between "the man [*sic*] who suffers" and "the mind which creates" (Eliot, 8). For him, the aim of art is transcendence. In a famous analogy he compares creativity to a chemical reaction in which the artist is a catalyst, an essential but invisible and unchanged agent. Reacting against the chummy biographical criticism of the nineteenth century, Eliot wants to purge literary studies of any interest in the social reality from which art springs.

In the 1920s both Woolf's and Eliot's ideas commanded attention simultaneously. Two early reviews of *A Room of One's Own* diametrically disagree about whether or not social context is an appropriate concern of literary criticism. The *New York Times Book Review* firmly rejected Woolf's argument, saying "The primum mobile [of art] must be genius itself. Jane Austen knew nobody and Georges Sand knew everybody, and Jane Austen was by far the greater, and there you have it" (2). But the reviewer in the *New York Herald-Tribune*, writing a few weeks earlier, supports Woolf:

> What, at first blush, could outrage more indecently our conceptions of how genius is nourished? A room, money—crass material positions! Is not fancy bred on the nectar of vicissitude, as the artist starves in his garret, his soul sped on its flight by the very privations to which his body is subjected? . . . More comfortable to assert that genius, like murder, will out; pleasanter for us who sit in snug houses to believe that privation, like a gaunt midwife, must preside at its [art's] birth. (7)

This review argues not only that the view of unstoppable genius feeds romantic fantasies about art but also that it absolves an indifferent society from the obligation of examining its material inequities. The comfortable illusion that Woolf shatters is that the material circumstances of art do not matter.

It is not only creativity that Woolf attempts to demystify but the nature of truth itself. Throughout the essay she treats with irony the notion of "some authentic fact" (41), "the essential oil of truth" (25), and "a nugget of pure truth to wrap up between the pages of your notebooks . . . [to] keep on the mantlepiece forever" (4). It is not only that her subject is too complex to yield such a neat conclusion, as the last quotation suggests. It is also that Woolf sees truth as subjective and contextual rather than abstract, objective, and universal. In this way she undermines traditional distinctions between fact and fiction. For Woolf, knowledge cannot be detached from knowers, who have specific human needs, values, and preconceptions, or from the conditions of knowing. One man's knowledge is another man's—or, rather, woman's—prejudice.

Alexander Pope announces that "most women have no character at all" (29), but, though enshrined in the British Museum, this confident pronouncement loses its authority in the narrator's investigation of male bias. In the same way the novels of John Galsworthy and Rudyard Kipling alienate women, despite their fame, because women bring to them a distinctively feminine consciousness: "Some of the finest works of our greatest living writers fall upon deaf ears. Do what she will a woman cannot find in them that fountain of perpetual life which the critics assure her is there. It is not only that they celebrate male virtues, enforce male values and describe the world of men; it is that the emotion with which these books are permeated is to a woman incomprehensible" (102). It is not that these novels should be universally appealing but that women are obtuse readers; rather, the novels do not speak to women as they speak to men. In the place of objective, universal truth Woolf sees gendered values and emotions.

To put the matter another way, all fact is fiction since it will always be, in some fashion, a human construction. There are many truths, some of them found in fiction, as she tells us at the opening of her essay: "Fiction here is likely to contain more truth than fact" (4). Thus along with Woolf's materialist view of creativity comes a contextual view of truth, one with an important strategic dimension, for if truth is subjective and relative then the outsider can claim the same authority for social observation and creative self-expression as the annointed expert. In *A Room of One's Own* this idea legitimizes the voice of the disenfranchised, lending a kind of philosophical grounding to feminist acts of re-vision.

A Room of One's Own addresses these issues with a series of questions. "Why are women poor?" Woolf wonders (28). Ironically, she says, "we burst out in scorn at the reprehensible poverty of our sex" (21). Can women's poverty be laid at the door of their own incapacity, as Desmond MacCarthy argues about their alleged lack of literary accomplishment? No, Woolf says, and drops the irony to consider what women have been doing instead: having children. "Making a fortune and bearing thirteen children—no human being could stand it," Woolf remarks (22). And even if women had been able to earn money, they could not keep it until 1870, when the Married Women's Property Act allowed them to keep their own wages rather than turn them over to their husbands: "It is only for the last forty-eight years that Mrs. Seton has had a penny of her own," Woolf reminds us (23). Woolf explains the inequality of men and women on the basis of social legislation and then goes on to show how this situation affected female consciousness. Because all her money would go to her husband, Mrs. Seton thinks, "to earn money, even if I could earn money, is not a matter that interests me very greatly. I had better leave it to my husband" (230). In this way the belief in women's subservience and entrenchment in the home becomes a self-fulfilling prophecy: unable keep her money, a woman gives up the idea of trying to earn it, and so she confirms the idea that her natural place is in the home.

Woolf's strategy for breaking through this apparently closed circuit is to contrast ideology with reality in order to expose the mystifications on which these social beliefs are based. Her recurring allusions to the legal status of women—the Infant Custody Act, the Married Women's Property Act, the restrictions on women's higher education, the achievement of suffrage—insist on the social construction of gender as the key explanation of women's status and achievements. Gender stereotypes, not female incapacity, keep women in their places—in the kitchen, the nursery, the drawing room, anywhere but a room of her own. Thus Woolf begins with an explanation of women's poverty that is built on the stereotype of women as vain and frivolous: "What had our mothers been doing that they had no wealth to leave us? Powdering their noses? Looking at shop windows? Flaunting in the sun at Monte Carlo?" (21). But she immediately explodes that myth with what we might call documentary evidence (remembering always that the status of "truth" is complex): a photograph of Mary Seton's unglamorous and careworn mother (21).

Woolf continues her investigation into the sociology of creativity with a second line of inquiry. She wonders "what effect poverty has on the mind; and what effect wealth has on the mind," extending her investigation of the relationship between the material conditions of life and human consciousness (24). Woolf imagines an experiment in which two groups of rats are fed different grades of milk, and the unsurprising result that this difference in the quality of nourishment produces rats of different health and vitality (53). This unflattering comparison of humans and caged rats serves a purpose. It undermines the romantic aura surrounding creativity; like the passages that compare university men to crayfish, it removes the protective coating of idealization from human activity so that it can be analyzed, not merely worshiped.

Playfully and ironically, the "ways of knowing" of science, traditionally a male domain, are appropriated for Woolf's feminist argument. She uses this question of nourishment to return briefly to the inequities between men's and women's education when she remembers the meager dinner at Fernham. The difference between men's and women's colleges appears as a kind of social experiment whose outcome is as predictable as a study of rats. The question of women's achievement, or alleged lack thereof, is not mysterious: it is the logical, even scientific, outcome of systematic deprivation. The men at Oxbridge eat a glorious dinner that burnishes their minds: "Thus by degrees was lit, halfway down the spine, which is the seat of the soul . . . the more profound, subtle, subterranean glow, which is the rich yellow flame of rational intercourse" (11). The women, in contrast, must settle for humbler fare, which does not produce such magical aftereffects. Their souls and conversations remain untransformed, for "the lamp in the spine does not light on beef and prunes" (18).

It is not only economic poverty but poverty of experience that affects women's achievements, particularly as writers. When Woolf contrasts the sweep of Tolstoy's life with the relative seclusion of George Eliot's, she concludes that *War and Peace* could only have been written by a man. The choice of Eliot as a contrast is particularly telling because she probably led the most liberated life of any Victorian woman writer—living in London apart from her family; acting as the de facto editor for the *Westminster Review*, one of the major journals of the day; and running away to the Continent with George Lewes, who was already married. Compared to the Brontës and Jane Austen, George Eliot lived a wildly unconventional life of passion and adventure. It is not that Woolf thinks that everyone should write *War and Peace* but that women's circumscribed experience limits the kind of writing they can do, whatever their talents or predilections.

Jane Austen may have been a great novelist despite knowing no one, as the *New York Times Book Review* critic claims, but she had no choice but to write the kinds of novels that she did. Once again, the idea of art as the spontaneous eruption of pure genius comes into question; the imagination cannot supply an entire realm of experience with which the author has no familiarity and which she has been told is diametrically opposed to her nature. The novel has been called the preeminent female form of fiction because it is based on human relationships and private life, which any woman could study without leaving the domestic sphere (although the example of *War and Peace* calls this simple definition into question). As Woolf recognizes, however, this special aptitude is a double-edged sword—a limitation as well as an opportunity—and one that feeds into female stereotypes. Thus Edward Fitzgerald's famous put-down of Jane Austen: "She is capital as far as she goes, but she never goes out of the parlour."[2]

Finally, Woolf reframes her second question to include psychological as well as material deprivation: "Surely it is time that the effect of discouragement upon the minds of the artist should be measured" (52–53). Woolf introduces her anecdote about the rat experiment in this way, drawing a continuum between the material and the psychological. We think of the difficulty of endowing Fernham, as opposed to Oxbridge, and the judgment implied about the relative importance of male and female education. Like the undernourished rat, the aspiring female artist faces a diet of disapprobation and condescension. She is "snubbed, slapped, lectured and exhorted" (55) rather than praised and encouraged. Woolf quotes Oscar Browning, famous Oxford don and literary critic, and W. R. Greg, celebrated Victorian journalist, as well as Desmond MacCarthy in her own day, all of whom insist on the inferiority of women. Woolf describes the effects of these opinions: "Her mind must have been strained and her vitality lowered by the need of opposing this, of disproving that" (55). In contrast, the writing of Mr. A has an ease and confidence that reflects a more wholesome diet: "One had a sense of physical well-being in the presence of this well-nourished, well-educated, free mind, which had never been thwarted or opposed, but had had full liberty from birth to stretch itself in whatever way it liked" (99).

These metaphors of vitality, strain, and nourishment derive from the body. They remind us of Woolf's insistence on the importance of material reality and of the connection between this reality and human consciousness. They remind us, too, of the female body itself and the social interpretation of sexual difference. Difference determines what the woman writer can and cannot do, what she is fed and how she is cared for, as if this were a matter of straightforward biology—just as dogs eat one kind of food and fish another. The body appears as an inescapable determinant of human existence; we can ignore its social meaning no more than we can ignore its physical claims and needs. While rejecting this social meaning of imputed inferiority, Woolf nevertheless keeps the female body before us, implying that a woman who writes is always a *woman* writer, never simply a writer.

7

Social Institutions and Creativity

How do the values and assumptions of patriarchy play themselves out? One of the chief ways is through social institutions, including those that do not seem to be political in an explicit or narrow sense. It is easy to see that granting men the vote while withholding it from women oppresses women, but, at first glance, a museum or a school would seem to be exempt from such concerns. One of Woolf's goals in *A Room of One's Own* is to show how even apparently innocent institutions such as Oxford, Cambridge, and the British Museum are in fact extensions of patriarchy, whatever other functions they perform. They appear in this essay as sites of privilege and power, as gateways at which the initiated are separated from the outsiders. They function in this way even more insidiously than suffrage legislation because they *appear* to exist to serve the disinterested pursuit of truth; they possess a cultural cachet that seems to mark them as precisely opposed to the hurly-burly and self-interest of politics. For Woolf, however, these institutions' emphasis on reason, learning, and the transcendent value of art masks a deep concern for perpetuating the status quo. As cultural critic Pierre Bourdieu says, "Art and cultural consumption are predisposed, consciously and deliberately or not, to fulfill a social function of legitimating social differences."[1] While the institutions might understand themselves as occupying a separate and opposite zone from political concerns, Woolf understands them as subtle extensions of other, more obvious forms of power.

Woolf's treatment of Oxbridge and the British Museum also extends the theme of the politics of space. These exalted spaces are shaped by the material and political conditions of society at large. And in a circular process they also reinforce and construct those material and political conditions as they police their borders, determining who may enter and under what conditions (at the British Museum, for instance, women may enter as readers but not as authors—they write none of the books on the shelves). Woolf subtly compares the politicized spaces in her essay—the common sitting room, the room of one's own, Oxbridge and the British Museum—both to show their common status as social products and to differentiate among their effects. Although we might like to think that we control the spaces we inhabit, Woolf suggests that they construct us as well: Oxbridge creates one kind of woman—the angry outsider—while a room of one's own creates another—the disinterested writer. The "room of one's own" takes on its full meaning only in the context of these other places. The narrator's movements represent a kind of journey of self-development through the alien and alienating spaces of public institutions into her own supportive environment.

Of these alien environments Oxbridge has the greater personal resonance for Woolf. The term is a common British neologism of the two great British universities. It suggests the united front these educational monoliths present. Given the diversity of educational institutions in the United States, even in the nineteenth century, it is difficult to realize the extraordinary tradition represented by these schools. Founded in the early twelfth century, they held a monopoly on university education in England until 1820. They were extremely selective in their admissions, based on social as well an intellectual qualifications. In addition to women, working-class and Jewish men were forbidden entrance until the twentieth century (Thomas Hardy's last novel, *Jude the Obscure*, vividly depicts the doomed efforts of a working-class youth to enter a university modeled on Oxford).

In their early days these universities resembled guilds or secret societies—a resemblance that persisted into Woolf's own era. An educational historian writes,

> The academic costumes and order of precedence were those of a caste system, albeit one that served to advance talent [Woolf would contend that vested interests are served as well.] The master was a brother within a mystery; he swore oaths, had privileges, and shared ritual equality with other masters. The guild limited membership to those whom they themselves alone approved. The inception of a new member was marked by processions, evening ceremonies, prayer, investiture, rings and the sharing of a banquet. It was a time of initiations, of beginning and end, and was marked by the many universal symbols of such a ritual passage.[2]

This description suggests the anthropological significance of university ceremonies: to annoint the initiates and to affirm the sacred boundaries of the group. The university's religious foundation gave an almost mystical quality to these proceedings; sacred mysteries are at stake, knowledge of which must be reserved for a handful of similar people in order to protect their magic. From this description it is easy to see why the universities resisted the efforts of women and other outsider groups to enter their space. The sacramental integrity of the guild was at stake.

Furthermore, education had always been part of the social apparatus that delineated and enforced sexual difference. In the nineteenth century battles raged over the consequences of education for women. Dr. Henry Maudsley, a noted physician with a private mental hospital for women, published a controversial article that argued that the mental exertion required by a serious education would imperil women's physical health, particularly their reproductive and nurturing capacities. He predicted dire consequences of this sapping of maternal energy: "For it would be an ill thing, if it should so happen, that we got the advantages of a quantity of female intellectual work at the price of a puny, enfeebled, and sickly race."[3]

Less drastic claims contrasted logic and reason with the intuition and emotion of an essential female nature. Learning Latin required women to unlearn their gender. Summarizing this Victorian attitude, Joan Burstyn says, "A learned woman . . . lost the very essence of her femininity."[4] When, toward the end of the nineteenth century, an older woman dined with a woman student at Cambridge, she reported, with relief, "My dear, she was a nice girl, with nice rosy cheeks, nice manners, and nicely dressed, and you wouldn't have thought she knew anything" (quoted in Williams, 183). Thus women's demands for higher education violated a profound, almost religious sense of institutional boundaries at the universities and deep-seated beliefs about gender in society at large.

Earlier we noted Woolf's sense of gender inferiority at having been excluded from institutionalized education when she asks her brother Thoby for a lecture on *Cymbeline*. We can understand the symbolic importance of this institution in *A Room of One's Own* more fully by considering its public and personal meanings for Woolf. Certainly the content of a university education was meant to distinguish a gentleman from his lower-class counterparts: knowledge of Latin and Greek had functioned as a class marker for centuries and continued to do so in Woolf's time. Of course, Woolf herself was very well educated in the classics, which conferred a class privilege on her as well. But her sense of disenfranchisement despite this points to the difference between knowledge itself and institutional accreditation. It was not only what they learned that privileged the men at Oxford and Cambridge: they were annointed with immediate prestige by posssessing a degree, marked as the best and brightest of their generation. They also had the opportunity to make contacts that would smooth their access into public life—what we call "networking" today. Certainly most students at Cambridge and Oxford were extremely capable and hard-working, but the cachet of a university degree carried what Bourdieu calls "cultural capital"—a kind of recognizable value that, like financial capital, can be traded on to increase the status of the bearer, independent of his virtues as an individual.

Looking at Woolf's immediate circle helps to clarify this phenomenon. First, most of her lifetime friends of the Bloomsbury Group were originally friends of her brother Thoby; educated at home, she had little opportunity for meeting people her own age and was forced to rely on him to provide her with a ready-made circle of friends. Most of Thoby's friends at Cambridge were members of a select society called the Cambridge Conversazione Society, or The Apostles, whose former members included Tennyson and Bertrand Russell. We can imagine what it would be like to see ourselves accepted into a tradition that included such luminaries; the sense of ability and cultural entitlement must have been powerful indeed. While we can imagine as well the pressure of trying to live up to such an exalted tradition, to an outsider such as Woolf it seemed, at times, an immense and unfair advantage.

Thoby's friends at Cambridge became well-known public figures: Clive Bell, the art critic; John Maynard Keynes, the internationally famous economist and later a lecturer at Cambridge; Desmond MacCarthy, literary journalist; Lytton Strachey, author, biographer, and essayist; and Leonard Woolf, civil servant, journalist, and socialist-activist. Other close, somewhat older friends with Cambridge degrees included the novelist E. M. Forster and the artist and impresario Roger Fry, who organized London's sensational Post-Impressionist Exhibition in 1910. MacCarthy, who succeeded merely in reviewing the most significant literature of the day for some of the most significant journals of the day, was considered in this circle to have left his potential unfulfilled. Even this brief list of occupations suggests the high levels of achievement to which university men aspired and which they often attained. With the expectations of accomplishment and the cultural accreditation provided by the university, these men moved easily into the larger world.

Thus Oxbridge carries a weight of meaning for Woolf, and she uses it to open her essay with some of the most memorable passages in feminist writing. For the narrator, Oxbridge is not the site of either disinterested learning or of social privilege but of exclusion. Her first experience is one of conflict: as she is thinking an angry beadle (a university functionary) chases her off the grass and drives away her thought. The incident is rich in symbolic implication. Literally straying from the gravel path, she has also strayed from woman's accepted place in the home when she enters these grounds, and she strays from woman's prescribed self-effacement when she expresses her thoughts in this essay. The fate of her thought is also important. She describes it vividly as a darting fish: "very exciting, and important; and as it darted and sank, and flashed hither and thither, [it] set up such a wash and tumult of ideas that it was impossible to sit still. It was thus that I found myself walking with extreme rapidity across a grass plot" (5–6).

The narrator's mental activity appears as compelling, exciting, alive—not the weak product of an inferior mind—and it is her thinking that sets her off the prescribed path into forbidden regions. The angry beadle scatters her thoughts; male authority, not female incapacity, blocks her intellectual progress. In these ways this incident portrays the power of patriarchy, but it is also takes a first step toward female achievement. The trespass is a demystifying act: the narrator's illicit presence calls attention to the absence of women at Oxbridge and to the double standard that keeps them out. It undoes the invisibility of women, revealing it as exclusion, just as the later reference to "blank spaces" on the bookshelves does. The narrator's trespass both reveals and fills the blank space at Oxbridge where women ought to be.

The narrator's next experience follows the same pattern. It is introduced, ironically, with a reflection on the conduciveness of the university to intellectual freedom: "the mind, freed from any contact with facts (unless one trespassed on the turf again), was at liberty to settle down with whatever meditation was in harmony with the moment" (6). The contrast between the hypothetical liberty of intellectual activity and the physical restraint just imposed on the narrator is striking. The narrator's description of the walled university as "a miraculous glass cabinet" suggests that Oxbridge's ease and freedom is something precious in the negative sense, something artificially protected from the real world (6). Moreover, even at the early moment in the essay it is possible to rewrite the contrast between quotidian "facts" and intellectual freedom as one between social reality and a kind of mystified privilege, which need not concern itself with restrictions of its movement or thinking since it remains exempt from them in this elite enclave.

These suggestions are subtle, but they are confirmed by the next section. The narrator remembers an essay by Charles Lamb, and her train of thought leads her to an anecdote involving the novelist Thackeray, the essayist Max Beerbohm, and Milton's famous poem *Lycidas*, the manuscript of which, along with one of Thackeray's novels, is held at the library. Then, posing a question about Thackeray's *Esmond* that could be resolved by examining the manuscript, the narrator finds herself at the library's door, only to be expelled by a librarian who tells her that women cannot enter the library without a male escort or a letter of introduction. Once again, the elite spaces of Oxbridge are protected at the expense of women—in this case a very well-educated woman, one who has read widely enough to drop several important literary names, who has enough specialized knowledge of literature to know where manuscripts are housed, and who asks sophisticated questions about Thackeray's use of an eighteenth-century prose style. Why has she been excluded? Clearly not because she is incapable of appreciating Oxbridge's intellectual riches. The distinction between knowledge and power is clear in this incident: her learning may be great, but it is irrelevant to the university, whose interest here lies in policing its borders.

At this point the angry narrator wanders by the chapel and has her vision of the Oxbridge dons as crayfish. It is her direct, personal experience of exclusion that grants her this satiric alternative perspective. These acts of rejection are painful, but they are also useful in clarifying the nature of the university a kind of elite social club. By the time she reaches the chapel, she claims that she has "no wish to enter had I the right" (8). She is stopped anyway. A feeling of "sour grapes" is at play here, but this moment also inaugurates the narrator's recognition of her status as an outsider. She has learned an important lesson at Oxbridge, but it has nothing to do with Milton's revisions of *Lycidas*. These early pages effectively contrast the ideal of Oxbridge as a repository of learning with the reality of Oxbridge as a social institution. It also revises the earlier contrast between intellectual freedom and "facts," showing that, for the narrator, it is precisely the politics of Oxbridge itself that derails her intellectual labors. For the narrator, Oxbridge is part of that inconvenient and distracting real world, with its power struggles and materialistic concerns; Oxbridge itself is a fact.

But, once more, this frustrating experience is a source of insight, for the narrator goes on to consider the incredible economic privilege that could produce such a miraculous glass box as Oxbridge. She imagines the "unending stream of gold and silver" that poured into the university, deliberately echoing the stream of consciousness in which her thought-fish darted when she entered the grounds, in another of the ironic contrasts between economic privilege and mental life (9). Now the narrator notices the concrete, material objects that define the campus: waiters, flowering window boxes, gramophones. Having been excluded from the places of learning and worship, the narrator finds other points of interest that reveal a different, less ethereal side of the unversity. The real world is very much present; Oxbridge appears as a privileged space, well-stocked with the appurtenances of a comfortable upper-class life. Perhaps it would have been safer to let her explore the library's manuscripts after all.

The climax of the narrator's movements, both physical and mental, occurs at lunch, where she is restored to her socially approved role as grateful guest rather than trespasser or satirist. The narrator observes that novelists seldom describe meals, but she violates this convention by providing a detailed and mouth-watering description of the elegant food at Oxbridge. This, too, might be considered a re-vision, a glimpse of a new woman's novel, in which the domestic sphere enters the foreground. Certainly Woolf herself lavished attention on party scenes in her depiction of woman's culture in *Mrs. Dalloway* and *To the Lighthouse*; the dinner-party scene in *To the Lighthouse*, including the succulent *bouef en daube* prepared by Mrs. Ramsay, is one of the most striking descriptions of fine dining in all of literature. To those of us accustomed to less inspiring institutional food, the Oxbridge meal sounds like a dream come true. Woolf's description is sensuous and evocative: the sole with its coverlet of cream sauce, the glasses flushing with their wines, the pudding rising from its sauce like Venus born from the waves in Botticelli's famous painting (colloquially known as "Venus on the Half-Shell," to continue the food metaphors)—even the lowly brussels sprout has been transformed into a rosebud.

The luncheon provides the opportunity to suggest another implication of the narrator's material observations. Partridges and wine feed the mind as they do the body, creating a feeling of well-being and ease that encourage mental freedom and creativity. In a passage noted earlier, the narrator says, "And thus by degrees was lit, halfway down the spine, which is the seat of the soul . . . the more profound, subtle, and subterranean glow, which is the rich yellow flame of rational intercourse" (11). Again, Woolf emphasizes the continuum of the material and the intellectual: from the spine to the soul, from the delicious food to the disembodied glow of rational intercourse. This passage introduces a series of metaphors involving light and flame that, because of their intangibility, might seem to discount the material in favor of the transcendent. But Woolf's point is that this perfect creative transcendence is the result of a process that begins in real life and in the body, that its intangibility requires a very tangible fuel in the form of food, money, space, and freedom. The rich yellow flame does not come out of nowhere; it blazes out by consuming the rich white cream of the luncheon and the heady privilege of university life.

In contrast, the meal at Fernham is plain and unappetizing. In place of sole, partridge, and pudding we find stringy beef, custard, and prunes. The sprouts, decidedly un-rose-like, are "curled and yellowed at the edge" (18). The lamp in the spine remains unlit. Alone with Mary Seton, the head of the college, the narrator hears the story of the founding of Fernham and the difficulty of raising even minimal resources. The story of Fernham differs from that of Oxbridge not only in its content—and that difference is dramatic—but also in its nature. The origin of Fernham can be tied to a particular date, 1860, more recent by centuries than the beginnings of Oxbridge, and it is peppered with the ordinary, concrete details of real and recent history: the *Saturday Review*, addressing envelopes, collecting the meager sum of £30,000. In contrast, we remember the almost lyrical account of Oxbridge's founding: "Somebody must have poured gold and silver out of a leathern purse into their ancient fists" (9). Oxbridge seems to have had an almost mythic origin, emerging from a picturesque medieval past so distant that the actual raising of money is entirely effaced. The story of its founding is more like a legend than like history, reflecting its current privileged status as the bastion of Britain's cultural legacy.

And yet Fernham has its attractions. It also diverges from Oxbridge in its lack of interest in policing its boundaries. The narrator simply walks into the garden, observing ironically, "unwisely, the door was left open and no beadles seemed about" (16). The gardens themselves are very different from the carefully manicured lawns at Oxbridge: they are "wild and open, and in the long grass, sprinkled and carelessly flung, were daffodils and bluebells, not orderly perhaps at the best of times, and now wind-blown and waving as they tugged at their roots" (17). A student tears across the grass—"would no one stop her?" (17). The entire impression is one of vitality and freedom, along with a little chaos. Unlike the Oxbridge men, "creased and crushed" like crayfish in their opulent aquarium, Fernham's inhabitants seem to benefit as well as suffer from their lack of a weighty history and importance (8). Again, Woolf finds value at the margins, where one is more free to stretch one's wings and improvise. Reflecting on the day's experience, the narrator observes, "I thought how unpleasant it is to be locked out; and I thought how it is worse perhaps to be locked in" (24). The university system has provided two important insights: first, the unequal opportunties for men and women, and, second, the benefits of exclusion. Fernham emerges not only as a poor-woman's Oxbridge but as an alternative and positive space, with different rules and values as well as a different menu.

These insights underlie the narrator's visit to the British Museum as well. Like Oxbridge, the British Museum is an institution of considerable cultural meaning. It, too, appears to stand above politics and economics, dedicated to the preservation of the past and of a disinterested culture. Vast and diverse, it seems to house a comprehensive collection of the world's artifacts, from Assyrian sculpture to the Rosetta stone to the Magna Carta to the only existing manuscript of *Beowulf*. The narrator likens its library, among the most extensive in the world, to a domed forehead—full, one imagines, of deep thoughts. What better place, then, to seek the truth about any subject? Accepting the British Museum's self-designation as a bastion of knowledge, regarding it as above "the strife of the tongue and the confusion of the body"

(26), the narrator goes there to consult "the learned and unprejudiced" in order to answer the questions prompted by her college visits—questions about the inequality of the sexes and the relationship between material and intellectual life (25). Armed with pencil and notebook, she seeks "the truth" (26).

But Woolf immediately begins to deconstruct these assumptions. As always, an apparently innocent description of the physical setting carries an important meaning. The narrator describes the street scenes around the museum: men shoveling coal and selling plants, refugees arriving with their luggage, people singing and shouting. With this she reminds us that even this august institution cannot really detach itself from the strife of the tongue and the confusion of the body. Indeed, she says, "London was like a machine. . . . The British Museum was another department of the factory" (25–26). This re-vision of the museum as part of the material side of modern life as well as a special sanctuary for the past prepares the reader for the investigation that follows.

The narrator discovers a wealth of information about women, but this compounds her difficulties. Its volume is overwhelming. Once again grotesque animal imagery expresses her alienation: she wishes for thousands of elephants, with their long life span, and spiders, with their many eyes, to digest all the information. Here begins the divergence between the narrator's imagined ideal truth and the knowledge contained in the British Museum: "How shall I ever find the grains of truth embedded in all this mass of paper?" (27), she asks. The narrator describes these works as "holding forth with . . . loquacity," finding that they are the productions of people who like to hear themselves talk. Rather than providing insight, these authors seem to have buried the truth under their words.

Then she makes another observation: the authors are all men. The idea of "learned and unprejudiced" scholars gives way to a much broader and less reliable collection of self-appointed experts—"agreeable essayists, light-fingered novelists, young men who have taken the M.A. degree; men who have taken no degree; men who have no apparent qualification save that they are not women" (27). Objectivity is reduced to a lack of direct knowledge: ironically, it is sexual difference, not information, evidence or logic, that empowers men to write about women. Their credentials are simply that they are not women, or, put another way, that they are men. Once again, as at Oxbridge, the narrator finds her own thoughts derailed by male authority: this time "an avalanche of books" interrupts her train of thought about why men are obsessed with the topic of women (28). Obediently, the narrator turns her attention from her own trespassing thoughts to the officially sanctioned knowledge before her. The comic list of topics that fall under the heading "Women and Poverty" continues the deconstruction of official knowledge. It is a long, chaotic, and contradictory list—"Weaker in moral sense than" followed shortly by "Idealism of"—and it concludes with a series of opinions by famous men ranging from Shakespeare to Oscar Browning, the Cambridge misogynist whom Woolf caricatures later in the essay. Unprejudiced learning has been replaced by an untidy array of opinions (28–29).

Instead of what we sometimes call book knowledge, the narrator finds another kind of knowledge through a very different process from the careful note-taking she anticipated. Daydreaming about a work entitled *The Mental, Moral, and Physical Inferiority of the Female Sex*, she makes two discoveries that grant her more insight into her question of women and fiction than all the scholarship in the British Museum. The first is the discovery that its author, Professor von X, is angry. Again, Woolf's strategy is to place this disembodied "Professor von X" into a real life, with speculations about his wife, his nurse maid, and his unfortunate appearance. No longer an impersonal expert, the professor becomes a living man with a specific and grim psychology that leaves him with a resentment of women. Continuing the light imagery of the meals at Oxbridge, the narrator discovers that these books "had been written in the red light of emotion and not in the white light of truth" (32–33). This emotion might be the professor's personal resentment of all the women who rejected him, as the narrator speculates, or it might be a less personal version of the same set of gender relations, in which men insist on women's inferiority to protect their own superiority.

Here Woolf introduces the metaphor of the women as mirrors, magnifying the image of men. It is not simply that these authors are ignorant about women because they are men, or entertain an abstract

prejudice against them; it is that their writing springs from their particular relationship to women. Far from being objective, they are
enmeshed in this relational structure of the gender. They write from a
deeply subjective and often self-serving position that can masquerade
as knowledge when it receives the imprimatur of the British Museum.
Even professors, apparently disinterested and mild-mannered, are part
of these power relations, both shaped by and perpetuating patriarchal
ideology: "Nobody in their senses could fail to detect the dominance
of the professor. His was the power and the money and the influence.
He was the proprietor of the paper and its editor and sub-editor" (33).

These writings about women serve the interests of patriarchy:
they continue to assert male superiority and maintain the unequal balance of power between the sexes, not only in their specific content
(which, we remember from Woolf's imaginary index, is sometimes
complimentary to women) but because men have seized the authority
of authorship along with the institutions that accredit and disseminate
ideas. Thus men have the power to define what women are. As the
narrator notes in passing, women do not write about men. The are not
granted the position of expert, and they can no more enter the British
Museum through their books than the narrator can enter the library at
Oxbridge. They are represented only by their absence: the "blank
spaces" where their books should be but are not.

At the same time, however, these observations reveal an instabil-
ity in the power relations between men and women. Hidden within
male superiority is female power. The relational structure of gender
roles makes them interdependent. We might revise the relationship
slightly to say that men depend on women's acceptance of their own
inferiority in order to shore up the male ego. The looking glass women
hold has "the magic and delicious power" of aggrandizing men; while
this power seems to do women little practical good, it nevertheless
reveals the dynamics of gender relations as more complex than they at
first appear (35). Master and slave are interdependent; neither can
exist without the other. If men define women on the pages of books,
women, it seems, have an equal if unofficial power to define men, one
on which men are entirely dependent and without which they are

insecure and ineffectual. "Is anger . . . the attendant sprite on power?" the narrator wonders (34).

Power breeds insecurity because the possibility of losing it always lurks around the corner, and because, paradoxically, it can only be held at the acquiesence of subordinates. The narrator provides a hyperbolic catalog of what could not have been accomplished without this enlargement of the male ego, such as "the glories of war" and the reigns of the czar and the kaiser—all achievements of power and violence. It also suggests that, without magnification, men would cease to be men, since the qualities that currently define them—including "all violent and heroic action"—would no longer be theirs (35–36). Far from being natural, gender relations appear as a strange conspiracy arranged among men and women that women have the power to subvert.

Thus the narrator's recognition of male anger opens up a series of insights that challenge received wisdom. Male needs, not male superiority, become the key aspect of gender relations; knowledge becomes prejudice and anxiety; objectivity becomes self-interest; and disinterested professors become patriarchs. Perhaps most surprising, far from being an assured and independent identity, masculinity is a dependent construction that needs women as its accomplice. The narrator also revises her own role: at first a humble supplicant seeking truth from the experts, she becomes a critic of the experts.

The narrator makes another discovery as well: she finds her own anger. She notices anger in her caricature of Professor von X, and she then represents her anger by drawing a raging fire over his portrait. Her anger is important because it represents another major insight into her topic, "Women and Fiction." After all, she is herself a woman writer, seeking material from which to compose a talk or essay. While the information in the British Museum disappoints her, she has discovered other insights from her own experience: when women write they confront debilitating verdicts from male authorities—verdicts that frustrate and enrage them. In a tradition of femininity that stresses passivity, charm, and delicacy, this aggressive and self-assertive emotion is taboo. The Angel in the House would never be angry, especially at a man. But faced with smug claims about the mental, moral, and physical inferiority of women, who would not be angry? This is the double bind of the woman writer, and it is undone as the narrator recovers female anger from its repression by patriarchal definitions of womanhood.

Although "the essential oil of truth" (25) has eluded her, the narrator has nevertheless found a "submerged truth" (31) in her doodle—and in what she had earlier dismissed as "the confusion of the body" (26). Reading the Professor's book, "my heart had leapt. My cheeks had burnt. I had flushed with anger" (32). The contrasts implied here suggest an entirely different structure of women's knowledge: fact versus fiction, scholarship versus the doodle, objectivity versus subjectivity, books versus the body. Confronting self-serving male prejudice, the woman writer turns to the authority of her own experience, to paraphrase the Wife of Bath from Chaucer's *Canterbury Tales*. Knowledge of women writers is not to be found in the patriarchal values of the British Museum, however revered and substantial that institution appears to be, but in women speaking for themselves.

Once again the alternate perspective of the outsider holds surprising promise. Frustrated by her difficulty in pursuing the nugget of truth, the narrator contrasts herself unfavorably with the Oxbridge undergraduate sitting next to her, who seems to be having no difficulty with his own research. But the contrast tells in the other direction as the scene develops: the undergraduate simply copies information while the narrator makes new discoveries, and he manages his inquiry so expertly because it conforms so neatly to preconceived ideas. The narrator observes, "The student who has been trained in research at Oxbridge has no doubt some method of shepherding his question past all distractions till it runs into its answer as a sheep runs into its pen" (28) (contrast this image to that of the darting fish at the beginning of the essay). The university training bought so dearly with streams of gold and silver succeeds only in replicating what is already known, while the narrator's untutored and emotional quest forges new ground. Such experiences as the narrator's, we can assume, should form the ground of the new history and the new psychology that the narrator repeatedly urges the students of Newnham to write. Not only their content but their method must be different, for if women are to tell their own story they must go beyond the received wisdom of books and explore the uncharted territory of felt experience and the female body.

The narrator's re-visioning is a new sort of truth, bound up in her own imagination and emotion; it is not the neat little nugget she hoped to find at the outset. Michel Foucault describes, in general terms, a narrator's process of discovery: "It seems to me that the possibility exists for fiction to function in truth, and for bringing it about that a true discourse engenders or 'manufactures' something that does not yet exist, that is, it fictions it. One 'fictions' history on the basis of a political reality that makes it true, one 'fictions' a politics not yet in existence on the basis of a historical truth."[5] The narrator "fictions" history—as, for instance, in her biographical explanations of Professor von X's resentment of women, or in her mock-history of civilization as the product of women's aggrandizing reflection of men—and her constructions gain credence because of the "political reality" of her own oppression. As the essay develops she "fictions" a politics of female inheritance and community, anchored by the mythical figure of Judith Shakespeare, from the "historical truth" of oppression as revealed in her discussions of women writers. Especially when history is the property of men, women's stories are a necessary fiction.

8

Female Creativity and Literary History

When the narrator leaves the British Museum for her own home in chapter 3 of *A Room of One's Own*, she likewise turns from male authority to female experience—the appropriate place to begin an investigation of women and fiction. Her exploratory journey has led her home, to her own bookshelf and her own sex. The narrator begins to construct a new body of knowledge and a new literary history, consisting not of Milton, Thackeray, and Charles Lamb but of the Duchess of Newcastle and Dorothy Osborne. According to Adrienne Rich, women need to break the hold of tradition because it silences them. Tradition itself is not the problem, however; it is the patriarchal nature of tradition. Tradition can in fact be enabling in several ways. It can show the woman writer that her conflicts about writing are not a purely personal problem but have been shared by many women as a function of patriarchal ideology. It can also provide useful models and examples and can authorize a woman's ambition by showing her that other women have written as well. Thus the narrator's counter-tradition is a potentially important part of a woman writer's development.

Woolf suggests the importance of this supportive tradition by exploring the damaging effects of male literary history on women writers. She writes of "Milton's bogey," suggesting a complex relationship of respect, estrangement, and inhibition that haunts women's reading of the male canon (114). Why should Milton be a bogey, or terrifying specter, for women? In part, simply because he is one of the giants of English literature, second perhaps only to Shakespeare in his totemic power. We remember that the Oxbridge library preserves the manuscript of his poem *Lycidas* and that Charles Lamb was so shocked that Milton had altered a line. For one thing, then, Milton is part of the patriarchal ideology that creates outsiders of women: Lamb may examine the manuscript, but the narrator may not. His manuscript remains a mystery, enshrined in hallowed precincts that open themselves only to initiates. For another, the attitude that *Lycidas* must have sprung full-blown from the mind of Milton, perfect and complete, perpetuates the cult of genius and suppresses the sociological and materialist questions that Woolf asks about creativity. In these ways Milton becomes a larger-than-life figure, his greatness increasing his awe-inspiring effect on women writers.

Woolf may also have had in mind the gender content of *Paradise Lost*, which has become the subject of debate among Milton scholars today. According to some feminist critics, Milton's poem reinforces patriarchal ideas about female inferiority in its treatment of Eve. Adam and Eve are

> Not equal, as their sex not equal seemed;
> For contemplation he and valor formed,
> For softness she and sweet attractive grace;
> He for God only, she for God in him. (Book 4: 296–99)

This passage posits stereotypical sexual differences in the original creation of men and women and grants Eve only a contingent relationship to God, through Adam. Elsewhere Eve appears in the familiar guise of the temptress, although perhaps she is an unwitting one, idolized by Adam because of her physical beauty, although he recognizes that her "nature . . . mind / And inward faculties" are "inferior" (Book 8: 541–42).

This version of Milton's poem remains controversial, and it does not address the gender beliefs of Milton's age. This portrait of Eve is nevertheless powerful. Invoking the spirit of God to both inspire and instruct him as the poem opens, Milton implies that God's voice speaks through him, granting his poem unassailable and divine authority. To question *Paradise Lost* is to question the voice of God. In speaking of Milton's bogey, Woolf attempts to demystify this aura of sanctity, turning a divinely inspired poet into a folkloric monster, much as she transformed the Oxbridge dons into crayfish. But the need to debunk Milton's authority reflects his influence over women's self-image. One can easily imagine the index at the British Museum containing the heading "Women, Milton's opinion of," yet another pronouncement about female incapacity. If the professors are patriarchs, the great writers may be as well.

The narrator, then, must seek a different tradition, for without one the woman writer is isolated, unsure, and at the mercy of patriarchal precepts. But when the narrator turns to women writers of the past, she unearths a series of conditions that have hampered female creativity. Not surprisingly, she finds that many of the conditions that kept women from endowing their colleges also apply to literary production. Financial dependence on fathers or husbands barred women from even the smallest escape from domestic responsibilities or the most innocent exposure to a wider life, and bearing children occupied all their energy. Woolf observes that, of her great nineteenth-century women writers—Austen, the Brontës, George Eliot— none had a child (66).

And, of course, patriarchal prejudices color the reception of women's work. A woman writer faced the double bind of being considered "only a woman" or "as good as a man," judged by standards that automatically denigrated her achievement (74). Small wonder women chose to remain anonymous or hid their identities behind male pseudonyms. All of Woolf's great nineteenth-century women writers did so: Austen's first novel was published by "A Lady," Emily and Charlotte Brontë wrote under the names Ellis and Currer Bell, and Mary Ann Evans remained George Eliot all her life. Explaining her and her sisters' use of pseudonyms, Charlotte Brontë wrote in her 1850 preface to *Wuthering Heights* and *Agnes Grey*,

> Averse to personal publicity, we veiled our names under those of Currer, Ellis and Acton Bell. . . . [W]e did not like to declare ourselves women, because—without at that time suspecting that our mode of writing and thinking was not what is called "feminine"—we had a vague impression that authoresses are liable to be looked on with prejudice; we had noticed how critics sometimes use for their chastisement the weapon of personality, and for their reward, a flattery which is not true praise.[1]

Strictures against female assertiveness compound the problem: "Anonymity runs in their blood," the narrator says, suggesting that women shrink from laying claim to their own words, that they lack the sense of personal authority implicit in the word "author" (50).

Moreover, for women authors, a destructive cycle of monstrosity and inhibition replaces this potentially ennobling male tradition—or at least it seems to at first glance. The relationship between the Duchess of Newcastle and Dorothy Osborne illustrates this point. The Duchess lacks the training she needs to think logically and has no sustaining intellectual community; increasingly isolated, she and her writings become wilder and wilder, until she, like Milton, becomes a "bogey" who discourages women from writing (62). To Dorothy Osborne, with "the makings of a writer in her" (63), the Duchess of Newcastle is a monstrous figure who confirms the idea that women should not write. Seeing her as a pathetic joke, Osborne writes, "If I should not sleep this fortnight I should not come to that"—that is, to writing books. Osborne writes only letters, a suitably private and unambitious form. If Osborne's husband had not been Jonathan Swift's personal secretary, we would probably not even have her letters. This is the negative tradition of women's writing—one that suppresses rather than encourages women's achievement and turns a potential writer into a woman who disdains public writing.

To drive this point home, Woolf invents one of her most famous creations, the figure of Judith Shakespeare. Jane Marcus speculates that she might have gotten the idea from the novel published in 1883 about Shakespeare's hypothetical daughter, entitled *Judith Shakespeare*, by William Black.[2] In any case, Woolf's invention has lived on to become one of the most famous parts of her essay (it is the only section anthologized in the *Norton Anthology of Literature by Women*). Judith Shakespeare is a fiction, invented to fill to blank spaces in female literary history, but, like much of the self-declared fiction in *A Room of One's Own*, she embodies a persuasive vision of history. Her story writes a real possibility into the historical record. As the narrator discovers in the British Museum, the lack of actual evidence about Elizabethan women means only that women's lives are often left undocumented or distorted by patriarchal assumptions, not that Judith Shakespeare or someone like her never existed. And she is a mythic figure as well—a kind of composite portrait that embodies all the tensions and frustrations of female creativity. She is a kind of Everywoman whose lack of a "real" existence does not mute her explanatory power.

The story of Judith Shakespeare is exemplary, revealing the consequences of sexual difference. Unlike her brother, who is free to study, seek sexual experience, leave home, and act and write, Judith confronts prohibitions wherever she turns. Her desire for guidance in the theater becomes derailed into an affair with a theater manager, followed by pregnancy and suicide—"who shall measure the heat and violence of the poet's heart when caught and tangled in a woman's body" (48). Her female body is the irreducible ground of her experience, and it destroys her creative potential, which is "caught" and "tangled" in it like a rabbit in a snare—or a fish on the line, to borrow Woolf's metaphor. Judith Shakespeare's life plays out the most tragic potential of the woman writer's story. The censure of the Duchess of Newcastle, the discouragement of Dorothy Osborne, and the overdetermined meanings of the female body are, in Woolf's imagination, intensified into archetype.

Although her experience is discouraging, it performs the important function of revising the meaning of women's alleged monstrosity. Although Dorothy Osborne regards the Duchess of Newcastle as crazy, she appears as a frustrated original talent through the lens of Judith Shakespeare's story. The bogey becomes a victim of prejudice; an apparently personal, individual history becomes a political one. Judith Shakespeare suggests the existence of an encoded tradition, one in which deviance might signal creativity. The narrator writes,

> When, however, one reads of a witch being ducked, of a woman possessed by devils, of a wise woman selling herbs, or even of a very remarkable man who had a mother, then I think we are on the track of a lost novelist, a suppressed poet, of some mute and inglorious Jane Austen, some Emily Brontë who dashed her brains out on the moor or mopped and mowed about the highways crazed with the torture that her gift had put her to. (49)

It is no surprise that, given the impediments to female self-expression, the literature that women do produce appears flawed. From the "caught and twisted" poet's heart issues writings that are similarly mangled: "twisted and deformed" (50) at one point in the text, "disfigured and deformed" at another (61), "deformed and twist-ed" at still another (69). This motif of deformity directly counters the notion of "natural" incapacity; it implies an unnatural development, something bent out of its organic shape. This deformity haunts the writings of many of the women Woolf describes: Lady Winchilsea, the Duchess of Newcastle, Charlotte Brontë. All of these women illustrate the narrator's assertion that art must consume whatever impediments it encounters to succeed fully. With these authors, the narrator says, resentment and anger distort creativity; Brontë's "indignation" creates awkward strains when it breaks into the the legitimate fictional world of *Jane Eyre* (69).

Woolf reconsiders the question of women's achievement else-where in the essay and turns her observations around: the problem may not rest exclusively with women's writing; it might have to do with the standards by which their writing is judged. In women's alleged disabilities, Woolf seeks a uniquely female aesthetic and tradi-tion. The first step in this process of re-vision is redefining gender as a relationship of difference and not of hierarchy. Women are not like men, but they are not inferior. In *Three Guineas* Woolf recommends that women cultivate "an attitude of complete indifference" to male standards, to turn a deaf ear to patriarchal ideology and to formulate their relationship to men "in difference," without attempting to conform to male standards (*Guineas*, 107). With no products or inventions to show for their labors, no competitions to determine the best mother or sister, no highly ornamental pots on their mantlepieces, women appear inadequate or invisible by male standards, their lives consumed with the evanescent business of cleaning house, raising children, giving parties.

The lesson of the British Museum is that, despite the reams of apparently expert analysis, women "remain at this moment almost unclassified," since traditional woman's work cannot be evaluated by male measures of achievement (85). Working from this experience, with this domestic tradition behind them, women writers will not create as men do. "They wrote as women write, not as men write" (74–75), the narrator says—and, moreover, "it would be a thousand pities if women wrote like men" (88). Woolf imagines opening up the field of culture and clearing a space for a uniquely female writing produced from that distinctive other place that women occupy in society. From sexual difference—those patriarchal definitions that demean and objectify women—Woolf fashions a female subject.

Given women's place in the world, we might expect women to write about different experiences from those of men: private life, personal relationships, the everyday business of being female. And it is not surprising that these concerns will appear superficial or unimportant in a male culture that valorizes public achievements. The narrator says,

> Speaking crudely, football and sport are "important"; the worship of fashion, the buying of clothes "trivial." And these values are inevitably transferred from life to fiction. This is an important book, the critic assumes, because it deals with war. This is an insignificant book because it deals with the feelings of women in a drawing-room. A scene in a battlefield is more important than a scene in a shop—everywhere and much more subtly the difference of value persists. (74)

In raising this question of what is intrinsically important—that is, in suggesting that what we consider to be intrinsically important is really important only in a specific context, in this case a patriarchal society—Woolf implicitly questions and revises her earlier comparison of George Eliot and Tolstoy. It might well be that Eliot's *individual* gifts as a writer would have flourished if she had lived more adventurously, but not because the Napoleanic Wars are always and automatically more interesting than the life of an ordinary English village. For Woolf, Eliot has failed to find her proper métier in village life (although many would disagree with this judgment), whereas for other writers this subject matter will be as fruitful as any sweeping public saga.

Jane Austen, one of the narrator's model authors, is a useful case study in this regard. Equally bound to the home—much more so, in fact, biographically—Austen nevertheless writes novels that Woolf considers nearly perfect: "Her gift and her circumstances matched each other completely" (68). Austen's novels focus exclusively on the private lives of the middle and upper classes; their great theme is marriage, and their scope at first seems limited. Austen herself called her novels a "little bit (two Inches wide) of Ivory," and, on occasion, this judgment has been taken up pejoratively by other critics.[3] We remember Edward Fitzgerald's famous aphorism, "She is capital as far as she goes; but she never goes out of the Parlour." Fitzgerald's comment is especially provocative given the politics of space that Woolf explores in her essay: relegated to the parlor, Austen is then criticized for never venturing out of it.

The parlor, however, can be reinterpreted in several ways as a site of essential human experience. Why should we see a concern for marriage, for instance, as self-indulgent? Certainly for women in the early nineteenth century, it could hardly have been more important, since it was their only real occupation and source of livelihood. Considering marriage trivial was a luxury of people who had other options—namely, men. We might also ask, with Woolf, why making money or fighting wars should take precedence over human relations. The parlor might hold all the drama and significance of the battlefield, only in a different key. And, perhaps most interesting, why might not the parlor raise the same issues as the public world? The bifurcation of private life in the home and public life in the marketplace is the illusory product of the ideology of separate spheres; it is not necessarily a factual description of human society. Thus public issues may express themselves in the parlor only in a somewhat encoded form. While we see few of Austen's characters actually working, they nevertheless live lives that are economically determined and are therefore intimately connected to the public world of allegedly important matters. Austen's two inches of ivory are deceptive: on them is inscribed an acerbic view of money, power, and social class that goes well beyond the parlor.

Against Fitzgerald's comment we can set W. H. Auden's witty defense of Austen in "Letter to Lord Byron":

> You could not shock her more than she shocks me;
> Beside her Joyce seems innocent as grass.
> It makes me most uncomfortable to see
> An English spinster of the middle class
> Describe the amorous effects of "brass,"
> Reveal so frankly and with such sobriety
> The economic basis of society.[4]

From women's imaginations, Woolf conceives of new narratives of what is now "unrecorded life": stories of match girls and old crones, of ancient ladies and their middle-aged daughters, whose experience eludes narrative conventions of a male tradition (89). This line of argument is especially cogent when we consider Woolf's concerted efforts to render the dramas of human consciousness that unfold just beneath the surface of ordinary private life in such works as *To the Lighthouse* and *Mrs. Dalloway*.

More audaciously Woolf imagines a female sentence, and by extension a literature that, in its formal and technical qualities, is distinctively female. The existing "common sentence"—a sort of template from which authors can develop an intelligible individual voice—is not universal but male, "unsuited for a woman's use" (76). Imitating it, women can only come to grief. Again, Woolf imagines Jane Austen as the ideal woman writer who invents "a perfectly natural, shapely sentence proper for her own use" (77). Exactly what does this female sentence consist of? It is difficult to say. Woolf's example of a male sentence does not entirely help, since it is also (and admittedly) quite Victorian—that is, tied to a specific age as well as to a gender—and a bit of a set-up. It is filled with abstract nouns—"grandeur," "satisfaction," "art," "truth," "beauty"—periodic in its structure and somewhat pompous (76). Although its weight and seriousness might suggest a stereotypical male posture, one could cull any of a hundred sentences from Thackeray, Dickens, or Balzac, to use Woolf's examples, and find a very different style.

Woolf has a different problem defining a woman's sentence in an essay on Dorothy Richardson. Praising Richardson for developing "a sentence which we might call the psychological sentence of the feminine gender," she specifies elasticity and delicacy as its special qualities—virtues not unrelated to the shapeliness of Austen's innovation. The emphasis is on beauty, not on power or authority. But she goes on to say, "It is a woman's sentence, but only in the sense that it is used to describe a woman's mind."[5] Here subject matter alone defines the sentence as feminine.

Although Woolf has a difficult time specifying the characteristics of a gendered sentence, she remains committed to the idea of a female literary form. The female body—an important part of Woolf's history of female experience—appears again in her meditations on the form of women's writing:

> The book has somehow to be adapted to the body, and at a venture one would say that women's books should be shorter, more concentrated, than those of men, and framed so that they do not need long hours of steady and uninterrupted work. For interruptions there will always be. Again, the nerves that feed the brain would seem to differ in men and women, and if you are going to make them work their best and hardest, you must find out what treatment suits them. (78)

This passage expresses Woolf's desire to ground creativity in the female body. She recognizes that the body is not automatically the site of unmediated and therefore authentic experience. Much of the essay analyzes the inescapable meanings that society imposes on it, such as the sexual double standard that defines Judith Shakespeare's pregnancy as shameful. But Woolf maintains the hope that, beneath these meanings, the body might provide the basis for a nonhierarchical difference, that it might serve as the origin of a distinctively female writing.

This utopian hope recurs in feminism, signaling the need to construct and legitimize an identity that can persuasively oppose patriarchal definitions of womanhood. In this turning to the body, Woolf anticipates the writing of some modern French feminist critics, particularly Hélène Cixous, who also seeks to elude patriarchal definitions with an appeal to the body. Cixous says of woman, "Her flesh speaks true. She lays herself bare. In fact, she physically materializes what she's thinking; she signifies it with her body. . . . She draws her story into history."[6] As in Woolf, the body is a medium through which a gendered language speaks. In Cixous, the body enacts language; in Woolf, language follows the body's form in some metaphorical way. When Cixous says, "She draws her story into history," we remember the narrator's discovery of her anger as both her own story and as the history of women writers in patriarchy. At these moments the body does seem to offer some hope of authenticity: it undoes the suppression of the narrator's feelings by presenting her with somatic symptoms, forcing her to read herself differently—indeed, to take herself, and not the books of experts, as her text.

Woolf's books in the shape of the body continue this hope, in a kind of sociobiology of creativity, determined by differences in nerves and the brain. Perhaps, like the story of Judith Shakespeare, this is a necessary myth, looking forward to a time when women can claim a literary voice without the strain of conflict and grievance—the body will simply speak. And yet perhaps because the idea that "anatomy is destiny" has so often rationalized women's oppression, Woolf also shies away from the body. Her book "framed for the body" is in fact framed for interruptions—that is, for the social circumstances of women's lives, not their physical forms. This confusion, like that surrounding Dorothy Richardson's female sentence, suggests the difficulty of using the body as a source of authentic womanhood.

Female Creativity and Literary History

But if Woolf cannot unproblematically establish a female literary form, she can still discover women's special talents by bringing different standards to bear. In addition to her explorations of female content and form, she also traces a distinctive kind of female authorship—we might call it style, orientation, or point of view—when she surveys women's writing. Just as blank spaces on a bookshelf tell one story of female creativity, so the impediments and liabilities of women's writing become a real tradition. One fills in the blanks with whatever is at hand. Thus from the claim that "anonymity runs in their blood" (50) comes the assertion that "Anon, who wrote so many poems without signing them, was often a woman" (49). The veiling and self-effacement of traditional femininity does not foreclose a literary tradition; they create a different kind of tradition from the male one, a rich lode of creativity stretching back to ballads and folksongs, that is simply not parceled up for the glory of individual authors.

Woolf's use of the names Mary Beton, Mary Seton, and Mary Carmichael is part of such a tradition. The names are from an old English ballad about the mistress of a king, who is to be put to death for bearing his illegitimate son:

> Last night there were four Marys
> Tonight there'll be but three.
> There was Mary Beton, and Mary Seton,
> And Mary Carmichael, and me.

The name Mary is only a step from "Anon," and, like that name, it is shared by several women who are somehow bound by their common identity. Woolf brings them to life in the new story of *A Room of One's Own* as an aunt, a college head, and a novelist—and perhaps we could say that the singer or the persona of the ballad, the Mary Hamilton who awaits her death, is a version of Judith Shakespeare. In a sense Woolf constructs a distinctively female *self*—more flexible, more communal, and less individualistic than conventional notions of identity. From their unique social position, Woolf imagines, women have evolved a particular way of being in the world, of addressing others, and of understanding themselves.

From the self-effacement and enforced anonymity of female experience come characteristics that Woolf recovers for their aesthetic value. What she likes about women is their "unconventionality," "subtlety," and "anonymity" (111). Forbidden direct self-assertion and self-expression, barred from the privileges of a well-fed body and mind, women are free to develop in other directions, to fashion a distinctive female aesthetic from these prohibitions. Woolf praises the suggestive power of women's writing, the offshoot of the indirection that women have been forced to practice. We remember the admonitions of the Angel in the House in "Professions for Women": "Be sympathetic; be tender; flatter; deceive; use all the arts and wiles of our sex" (235). In *A Room of One's Own* Woolf imagines these arts and wiles turned to artistic benefit, shaping a more flexible, less assertive authorial voice and a more unstructured, allusive narrative. While in *A Room of One's Own* she regrets the fact that Dorothy Osborne did not write novels, in the essays "Dorothy Osborne's Letters" and "Mme de Sévigné" she celebrates the easy, unassuming postures these women adopt in their letters—in part because they did not see themselves as potentially famous artists writing for posterity. Mme de Sévigné is especially prized: she relinquishes her pen to other hands, who interpolate her letters with their own thoughts in an ideal of communal rather than egotistical authorship—a sort of party in prose.

These ideas are not simply claims that Woolf makes for the sake of argument; they come very close to representing her aesthetic philosophy. Attempting to distinguish her own technical experiments from those of other modernist writers, Woolf stresses the importance of avoiding "the damned egotistical self; which ruins Joyce and [Dorothy] Richardson to my mind: is one pliant and rich enough to provide a wall for the book from oneself" (*Diary*, 2: 14). Woolf's inclusion of Dorothy Richardson in this critique suggests that it is not strictly a matter of biology. Nevertheless, Woolf frequently associates this dispersion of the ego with women's writing, including her own. Her experiments with narrative and characterization direct themselves to the issue of ego, as the titles of two studies of her fiction suggest: *The World without a Self* and *Fables of Anon*. Critics have repeatedly recognized her attempts to decentralize narrative authority and create characters whose diffuse states of consciousnesses resist the focus and rigidity of "that damned egotistical self." In *A Room of One's Own* Woolf claims that these aesthetic experiments are gendered, growing logically from women's social role.

In this process of re-visioning Woolf also reverses the earlier contrast between male and female achievement. Whereas at Oxbridge the delicious meal bespoke the mental comfort and freedom needed for unimpeded creation, Woolf finds liabilities in that very privilege: a kind of smugness, a certainty, a self-consciousness about one's own abilities that mars male fiction. Reexamining male fiction with a critical eye, Woolf stacks the deck with her choice of Galsworthy and especially Kipling as representatives of masculine art—although, in fairness to her argument, she never claims that they are representative of all male writers, only that they display the aesthetic qualities of masculinity with special clarity.

In both his subject matter and his insistence on the grandeur of his concerns, Kipling reveals the unexpected dangers of being a male writing in a male culture. Unintentionally, his writing sounds like a parody of patriarchal values: "So with Mr. Kipling's officers who turn their backs; and his Sowers who sow the Seed; and his Men who are alone with their Work; and the Flag—one blushes at all these capital letters as if one had been caught eavesdropping at some purely masculine orgy" (102). Kipling's reverential treatment of the British Empire matches the imperialism of his literary style, with its assertive capital letters and its certainty that its values are the only ones, to be imposed on the reader. Kipling's "Flag" insists that it is the only flag, a kind of archetype that should evoke in every reader the awe of a colonial subject. Audaciously, Woolf construes patriarchy as a set of values and attitudes stretching from prose style to international politics. When she praises women for being able to look at a "very fine negress" (50) without wishing to make an Englishwoman out of her, she describes a female subject who is both exempt from the political impulses of imperialism and sensitive enough to difference—perhaps a legacy of her experience as Other to the male norm—to preserve the distinctiveness of other people, whether in social life or in fiction (52).

Woolf continues this train of thought in her hypothetical example of the male novelist Mr. A: "Then Alan got up and the shadow of Alan at once obliterated Phoebe. For Alan had views and Phoebe was quenched in the flood of his views" (100). The male character of a male author takes the floor, and the female character becomes a mere cipher. It is the "I" of this man's book—the self-assured male ego that asserts itself through its fiction, "hard as a nut, and polished for centuries by good teaching and good feeding" (100)—on which the novel, ironically, founders. Like the arm-waving beadle who chases the narrator off the grass, like Milton's bogey, which shuts out the view, the authorial "I" plants itself squarely in the middle of the novel, forcing the reader to dodge "this way and that to catch a glimpse of the landscape behind it" (99). Ironically, with all the material advantages, Mr. A's male ego does not create; it succeeds only in reproducing itself, in substituting its own image for an imaginative reality, in colonizing the space of fiction. Applying different standards, Woolf has not only cast light on women's writing but has reevaluated male writing as well. If women's liabilities can be seen as virtues, male privilege can also become a liability. For the woman reader, Woolf says, male prose is as limited as men have judged female prose: "The emotion with which these books are permeated is to a woman incomprehensible" (102).

As Woolf teases out the qualities that distinguish women's writing, the impossible emerges: a female tradition. If half of everything signed "Anon" was written by a woman, then it is a substantial tradition indeed. Woolf insists that the woman writer "is an inheritor as well as an originator" (109), the product of the women who have come before her. If there are only a handful of great women novelists, by traditional measures, then she will have to trace her lineage along a different path, through anonymous authors, letter writers, witches, female bogeys like the Duchess of Newcastle, and mythical creations like Judith Shakespeare. Paradoxically, it is their very marginality that makes them such useful precursors, for their example steers women writers away from the egotism of male authorship.

This acceptance of marginality produces one of the most appealing aspects of Woolf's essay: her attempt to bridge the gap between what we might call the modern career woman, with her insistence on a public place in the world, and the women of the past. Woolf seeks a historical continuity that will respect differences in female experience. She does not attempt to construct a politically correct feminism that might, for instance, assert that all women should work outside the home or write novels instead of letters, nor does she wish to polarize women if their lives are different. In Woolf's famous formulation, "We think back through our mothers if we are women" (76). She ties together the public achievements of women like herself and the domestic values of earlier generations. With its connotations of nurturance and support, this formulation also humanizes literary inheritance.

Ancestors do more than simply provide technical models for aspiring writers or symbolize particular aesthetic philosophies—indeed, they may do nothing of the sort, for they may not even be writers. Instead, this female tradition—with distinct values, attitudes, and even modes of selfhood—sustains a woman writing in a male world, giving her a kind of affirmation of identity like that which a mother ideally gives to her child. There is a kind of intimacy between ancestor and inheritor. Woolf's essay has given rise to the term "foremother," widely used in feminist criticism, to suggest the gendered nature of literary inheritance and the importance of a female ancestor who nourishes her inheritor.

If providing nurturance rather than literary models is the central function of the foremother, it does not matter whether she writes at all—or even whether she exists. Thus Judith Shakespeare becomes a powerful inspiration to her inheritors because her fictional life acts out so many of the tensions and contradictions they experience. At the essay's end she becomes a kind of spirit of female creativity who inhabits all women. In this mythopoetic conception "the dead poet who was Shakespeare's sister will put on the body which she has so often laid down. Drawing her life from the lives of the unknown who were her forerunners, as her brother did before her, she will be born" (114). This lyrical conclusion suggests the special dynamics of female literary history as Woolf understands them. Judith Shakespeare is both a foremother of future writers and the spirit who is reborn in the future, when the potential she symbolizes is realized by modern women.

The process is not one of linear influence but of circularity and mutuality. The modern writer is legitimized and affirmed by her foremother, and the foremother is resurrected by the modern writer, who confirms her potential and perhaps rediscovers her. This is what Woolf does with writers such as Dorothy Osborne and the Duchess of Newcastle: their examples provide her with a female aesthetic of self-effacement and anonymity, and she brings their now-obscure names back to life. The roles of mother and daughter are not fixed but pass back and forth between ancestor and inheritor, as each gives birth to and emerges from the other's work.

The novel by Mary Carmichael crystallizes the possibilities of Woolf's female aesthetic and tradition. It is worth noting that the name Mary Carmichael again blurs the boundary between fiction and fact: she is both a character from the ballad and a real person, the author of a 1928 novel, *Love's Creation*, which includes a scene of two women in a laboratory like the "Chloe liked Olivia" scene.[7] We might, then, consider Woolf's choice of this name as another instance of the shared, diffuse identity of women writers. The novel of Woolf's Mary Carmichael itself declares its allegiance to new ways of seeing and new forms of expression; both "sentence" and "sequence" disrupt the reader's expectations (81). While this disruption makes Woolf's narrator uncomfortable, she does not write it off as a technical flaw. Instead it may be the mark of sexual difference, proceeding from a different angle of vision and requiring different standards. Of this disruption the narrator speculates, "Perhaps she had done this unconsciously, merely giving things their natural order, as a woman would, if she wrote like a woman" (91). One effect of this difference is to unseat the critic, who must dispense with her stock phrases of praise or blame in order to understand this new phenomenon. Rather than feeling "serious and profound and humane" as she is accustomed to she wonders if she is "merely lazy minded and conventional into the bargain" in her inability to catch the rhythm of Mary's narrative (92–93).

No less unsettling is the novel's subject matter. In one of the most famous passages of *A Room of One's Own* Woolf offers the reader a theme of startling originality: "Chloe liked Olivia" (82). This simple scenario in fact contains radical possibilities. In a general way, Woolf claims, with much justice, that women are not represented in relation to each other in fiction: they are the wives, lovers, daughters, and sisters of men, but their important relationships are never with women (or at least they were not in 1929). In this new scenario the characterization of women will certainly change; they will be "much more various and complicated" than in their previous contingent condition (83). Moreover, this simple three-word sentence disrupts one of the most basic plots in literature, the love story, and replaces it with an entirely new subject. What story will follow from this proposition? There are no ready-made formulas for developing the situation of one woman liking another, no equivalent to "boy meets girl, boy loses girl, boy gets girl." No matter what the nature of the liking—and, as we shall see, Woolf leaves this deliberately ambiguous—no conventions exist for describing it.

It is even possible to regard this new situation as a drastic rewriting of the social structure, for female contingency is not limited to novels. It is worth glancing at recent feminist theory to understand why this simple statement has such radical implications. In an influential article anthropologist Gayle Rubin has argued that, in the basic social structure in Western societies, women take the part of objects, commodities, or gifts that are circulated among men. Men exchange commodities; women are exchanged. To use a simple example, women are "given away" in marriage from father to husband; they do not give themselves away, nor are men given away either by other men or by women. Rubin uses the expression "the traffic in women" to mean "that men have certain rights in their female kin, and that women do not have the same rights either to themselves or to their male kin."[8] We might consider this another definition of patriarchy: women exist as the property of men, and their primary relationships are to their owners. Such an arrangement clearly anchors male power by granting men the privilege of ownership and by keeping women at arm's length from each other.

Given these assumptions, it is small wonder that a relationship between women, unmediated by a male subject, would be perceived as profoundly subversive; it would upset the entire power structure on which sexual difference rests. French feminist critic Luce Irigaray considers this possibility in an essay whose title has been translated as "Commodities among Themselves" and, more colloquially, "The Goods Get Together": *"But what if these 'commodities' refused to go 'to market'? What if they maintained 'another' kind of commerce, among themselves?"*[9] This comical picture of commodities with minds of their own underscores the dramatic, destabilizing change Irigaray envisions: by entering into relationships with each other, women can refuse their status as objects. When Woolf imagines Chloe liking Olivia, she has something like this in mind: they have important lives outside of their domestic roles, and they are not defined and controlled by their relationships to men. Information about their private lives—once the only information at all—is given as an aside; the narrator is not completely sure how many children one of them has.

In celebrating the friendship of Chloe and Olivia as "more varied and lasting because it will be less personal" (since it takes place in a laboratory) and in giving one of the women a family, Woolf suggests that this relationship is purely platonic (84). But other clues suggest that Woolf may have had in mind the equally radical possibility of a lesbian attachment. In the draft of *A Room of One's Own* this possibility is raised more pointedly, although still implicitly, by the suggestive sexual imagery that surrounds the narrator's reading of this passage. Even in the published version Woolf mentions Sir Charles Biron, who was the presiding magistrate at the obscenity trial of Radclyffe Hall's lesbian novel *The Well of Loneliness*, which was taking place as Woolf was revising her talks into the final manuscript. (There may be an added connection in the fact that Hall was a descendent of William Shakespeare, whose reputation survived his homosexual sonnets, while Hall was persecuted in what might be seen as another example of the sexual double standard [Marcus, 166].) Woolf herself had been involved in Hall's defense as early as September 1928, before she delivered the talks, when she wrote a letter to the *Nation & Athenaeum* protesting the book's suppression. We might remember, too, that Woolf was at the time deeply involved with Vita Sackville-West: the two were sexual partners and supportive readers for each other, and Woolf's intimate, fanciful portrait of Sackville-West in

Orlando had been published less than two weeks before her trip to Cambridge.

Anticipating the publication of *A Room of One's Own,* Woolf fears not only being "attacked for a feminist" but "hinted at for a sapphist" (*Diary,* 3: 262)—that is, a lesbian (after the Greek poet Sappho, who celebrated lesbian love). The reference to Charles Biron may be taken as an example of male heterosexual paranoia—men will see women together in any situation as lesbians because that is the most threatening and deviant possibility they can imagine—or as a subtext that subtly reinterprets the essay's explicit message. Has the thought of this obscenity prosecutor frightened the narrator into censoring Mary Carmichael's novel? Is the relationship really "less personal"—and less personal than what? In the published essay Woolf leaves these matters entirely ambiguous, but even to raise indirectly the subject matter of *The Well of Loneliness* is to remind her readers that a new woman's novel has already been written. Some of Woolf's most famous novels, such as *Mrs. Dalloway* and *To the Lighthouse,* deal with erotic bonds between women, although not with what we would today call lesbian relationships. The idea that women might prefer each other to men, might not need men at all, would certainly be a different story. For whatever reason, Woolf was unwilling to tell the story outright, but it certainly formed part of her thinking as she composed the essay.

Finally, Mary Carmichael's novel takes its place in the female tradition. The narrator approaches her "as the descendent of all those other women whose circumstances I have been glancing at . . . [to] see what she inherits of their characteristics and restrictions" (80). We have seen that she has altered the sentence, as Jane Austen did, and the sequence as well. Despite her modern cadences, the narrator tells us, she retains some taboos from earlier times: a reticence about sexuality and an investment in the class system (88). Because of her name, she also takes her place in the tradition of "Anon," focal point for the unrecorded lives of obscure women, as her identity intersects with those of the other Marys in the ballad.

After a fashion, she is also a descendent of Mary Beton, the aunt who leaves the narrator £500. In a very indirect way, we might imagine Mary Carmichael with her own Aunt Mary, inheriting the money that gives her the leisure to write *Life's Adventures*. Somewhat more directly, we see her as the successful inheritor of Mary Beton, who falls from a horse in India. When she approaches a complication in her novel the narrator uses the metaphor of horseback-riding to suggest Mary Carmichael's difficulties and to urge her on. As Mary approaches the metaphorical jump, the narrator notices "the bishops and the deans, the doctors and the professors, the patriarchs and the pedagogues" crowding at the fence, giving her instructions and injunctions: "Fellows and scholars only allowed on the grass! Ladies not admitted without a letter of introduction! Aspiring and graceful female novelists this way" (93). As Mary Carmichael sails over the fence she not only succeeds in her own writing but supplies a new ending to Mary Beton's story of failure and destruction. Her experience may also imply a new meaning for the old story: Perhaps Mary Beton was startled by the patriarchs as she attempted to stretch her wings and take a jump. The connections between Mary Beton, generous aunt exiled to India as a handmaiden of Empire, and Mary Carmichael, the modern woman writer who follows her own vision, reveal the mutuality and reflexiveness of female literary history. The foremother and daughter comment on and complete each other. Empowered by the mother's legacy—financial or otherwise—the daughter both surpasses and pays homage to her partial achievement, recovering her from obscurity.

9

The Essay as Novel: Technique in *A Room of One's Own*

It is no accident that Jorge Luis Borges did the Spanish translation of *A Room of One's Own*, since the twists and turns of Woolf's narrative, her creation of a shadowy persona, and her heavy use of irony resemble some of Borges's fictional techniques. For the first-time reader, *A Room of One's Own* can be a confusing narrative. As Marcia Folsom has observed, students sometimes find it "idiosyncratic and exasperating" because it does not develop in a linear way, offering propositions, supporting them with evidence, and then moving logically to the next step (Folsom, 255). The essay meanders, circling around its concerns without, apparently, lighting for long on any one conclusion, losing its way in all sorts of tangents. Readers may wonder why Woolf's essay has been so revered, since it violates many sacred tenets of expository writing.

Woolf is not, however, simply an artist whose imagination is so highly developed that she cannot think rationally. Her essay follows a powerful if subtle strategy that reflects her ideas about male and female writing. Its rhetorical effect of indirection makes more sense when we recall her rejection of male authority in authors such as Kipling, Mr. A, and Professor von X. Woolf does not wish to make a conventional argument because, first, she wishes to avoid the coercive, definitive voice of patriarchy. Remembering that the apparently objective truth housed in the British Museum turned out to be little more than prejudice, we can appreciate the disclaimer with which she begins her investigation: "When a subject is highly controversial—and any question about sex is that—one cannot hope to tell the truth. One can only show how one came to hold whatever opinion one does hold. One can only give one's audience the chance of drawing their own conclusions as they observe the limitations, the prejudices, the idiosyncrasies of the speaker" (4).

Of course, Woolf is being somewhat disingenuous here: she makes a forceful if unconventional argument that does not exactly grant the audience total freedom to form its own conclusions. On the other hand, in creating her fictional narrator to take over the story, Woolf puts aside her reputation as one of England's greatest novelists—which, after all, is why she was invited to speak in the first place. Her audience may feel more free to adopt a critical perspective on the arguments of Mary Beton than on those of Virginia Woolf. Obviously, Woolf has a point of view, but she wants active readers who will engage in her argument rather than swallow it whole, without reflection. She wants to entice and persuade, not coerce or brainwash.

In rendering the narrator's roundabout thought process, the narrative emphasizes the subjective nature of the argument. We see it not as a finished, air-tight, abstract syllogism but as the product of a thinking mind, formed through specific experiences. In a sense, then, the narrative reflects Woolf's emphasis on the sociology of art: the material context of the narrator's thinking is shown to affect her ideas and attitudes. The section on the British Museum is especially instructive. We should contrast the narrator's frank admission of her anger, and her visible if unacknowledged suppression of it, with the smooth facade of objective knowledge presented, at first glance, by Professor von X's diatribe against women. The point of this contrast is that, at least in theory, Professor von X's conclusions are no less subjective than the narrator's (although we cannot help but believe that they are a good deal less reliable), and they are much more insidious because they masquerade as fact.

In many ways the essay establishes a kind of informality that is a deliberate if implicit contrast to the university lecture on *Cymbeline* Woolf desired as an aspiring young writer. It begins not with an assertion but with a qualification: "But" (3). Starting in medias res, the essay takes on a conversational, unfinished quality. We seem to have caught Woolf in the midst of a personal meditation. The usual balance of power between essayist and reader, lecturer and listener, has changed. We seem on a more equal, more intimate footing. She simply talks to us; she does not make pronouncements. Probably we should not write down every word she says, like overdutiful students, since she has already changed her mind in the first sentence. With this first word Woolf refuses the idea of "a nugget of truth"—simple, single, and authoritative. "But" calls into question what has come before, opening the possibility of dialogue, of multiple perspectives, of re-visioning. It signals to us that the essay will not proceed directly but will employ tactics of circling around and rethinking its own points in order to arrive at a complex truth.

This "but" recurs at crucial points in the essay. When the narrator praises the ease of Mr. A's writing in contrast to Mary Carmichael's unconventional prose, she circles around her reservations with several unfinished sentences beginning with "but," finally concluding, "But—I am bored!" (100). Although the weight of Woolf's argument is certainly on the boredom, she does not instantly dismiss Mr. A's facility, recognizing the palpable advantages of his familiar, confident style. It is worth noting, too, that the narrator's objections are not couched in abstract or objective terms. They are quite frankly the statement of a subjective reaction. The essay's final sentence on the second coming of Judith Shakespeare also begins with "but": "But I maintain that she would come if we worked for her, and that so to work, even in poverty and obscurity, is worth while" (114). This "but" registers a hope in the face of oppression; it contains, in a sense, the thrust of Woolf's argument that, despite all impediments, female creativity survives.

In a sense the entire female tradition Woolf uncovers, or constructs, grows out of this word "but" and the willingness it conveys to rethink the meaning of evidence or common wisdom. Dorothy Osborne wrote only letters, but what a letter writer she was; she regarded the Duchess of Newcastle as demented, but she retained and expressed her own gift for writing. These "buts" are nodes of re-vision in the essay, moments when the argument shifts gears in order to fill in a blank space or to search out an unrealized possibility.

In the same way, she rejects the conventional closing of a speech, the "peroration." The word has two related but different meanings on which Woolf plays. The first is the recapitulation at the end of the speech, a conclusion that emphasizes the main points. The second is a pretentious, grandiloquent speech or harangue. According to Woolf's theory of gendered writing, the second kind of peroration would be a distinctively male rhetoric, the climax of the formal, definitive lecture. Even the first, apparently neutral meaning is problematic. For one thing, peroration sounds too pompous to mean a simple summary; like patriarchal prejudice disguised as fact, this word pretends to be more than it is in order to impress an audience. Also, simply because it is so conventional a form, Woolf imagines that its content must be conventional as well. It will take new forms of address, a new rhetoric, to subvert the old structures of authority of the lecture. The only perorations she can imagine are sexist clichés. Women should remember their responsibilities and be spiritual; since, according to received wisdom, women dislike women, her essay should end with "something particularly disagreeable" (111). Apparently the authority invested in the peroration can make a patriarch out of any speaker.

In this essay, however, Chloe likes Olivia, so *that* peroration can be deployed ironically and then abandoned. The closing message will have to be different. Woolf concludes, unpretentiously, that "it is much more important to be oneself than anything else," and, subjectively, that "I often like women, I like their unconventionality. I like their subtlety. I like their anonymity" (111). In condensed form, this is the essential point: that women are different, and that this difference is valuable. The conclusion echoes the rest of the essay but without the fanfare of a peroration. And the final paragraphs dispense altogether with the format of the essay in favor of fiction, when Woolf resurrects Judith Shakespeare as the inspiration for women writers of the present and future. Through the lyrical, suggestive prose of fiction Woolf gives weight to her conclusion.

Given Woolf's deconstruction of the objectivity of history, it is not surprising that she would turn to fiction as a model of technique as well as a source of insight. Throughout this study I have been referring to Woolf's book as an essay; one might just as accurately describe it as a novel. I have said that Woolf called the early drafts of *The Years* a novel-essay; *A Room of One's Own* could be called the same thing, except that instead of alternating fiction and history in separate chapters it integrates them in a complex narrative strategy. If truth is multiple and elusive, it might be more easily pursued through the subtlety of fiction than through argument and logic. Woolf approaches her subject—women and fiction—by dramatizing it as if it were the plot of a novel. The essay acts out the tendencies of women writers and their work, using the narrator as a fictional character and recapitulating its arguments about women writers in the narrator's complicated attempts to tell her own story.

Woolf uses a number of the techniques of fiction to achieve subtlety and indirection throughout the essay. The most notable and dramatic is her use of a fictional narrator. She begins the essay in something like her own voice—at least that is what she seems to do. But after only a few paragraphs she complicates the address, saying, "'I' is only a convenient term for somebody who has no real being" (4). She further complicates the identity of authorship a moment later, saying parenthetically, "Call me Mary Beton, Mary Seton, Mary Carmichael or by any name you please—it is not a matter of any importance" (5). Virginia Woolf, arguably the foremost authority on women and fiction, has replaced herself with an unreal "I" who might be a version of several fictional women in an old English ballad. In doing so she has created a fictional character in the person of the narrator, who not only reports the difficulties and abilities of women writers but acts them out. She is herself a woman writer, and her first impulse is to veil herself behind fiction and ballads, to sign the essay "Anon." Like the women she writes about, she herself is "terribly accustomed to concealment and suppression" (84).

Her argument, she says, consists of "what chance has floated to my feet" rather than her conscious thoughts or intentions (75). She dismisses the contrasting images of the meals at Oxbridge and Fernham as "disjointed and disconnected and nonsensical" (19), denying the significance of her own insight. Indeed, she hopes that by talking about these disjointed images she will exorcise them, for they seem so meaningless that she expects them to "fade and crumble like the head of the dead king when they opened the coffin at Windsor" (19). Like Dorothy Osborne, the narrator resists the self-assertion of authorship, preferring to devalue her intuitions rather than pursue them. We might regard her as a case history in oppression, obligingly forgetting her idea about women and fiction when she is chased by the beadle and internalizing prohibitions against women when she says she has no desire to enter the chapel, having already been banished from the grass and the library. Through her narration we see the consequences of patriarchy on women's minds. Having promised to "develop in your presence as fully and freely as I can the train of thought which led me to think this" (4), she says a few paragraphs later, "I will not trouble you with that thought now" (5). In a sense both statements are accurate. This *is* as freely and fully as she can develop her ideas, given the social disapprobation that attends a woman who speaks her mind.

Thus what appears to be a rambling, inconclusive style is in fact a conscious strategy of representation and argument. The narrator's digressions, disclaimers, and evasions are significant. They act out the anxieties of the woman writer and reveal her ideas, although in a covert way. We should be alert to the fact that we are reading a kind of cover story or a palimpsest, which Sandra Gilbert and Susan Gubar describe this way: "In effect, . . . women have created submerged meanings, meanings hidden within or behind the more accessible, 'public' content of their works" (Gilbert and Gubar 1979, 72). The narrator does not efface herself so much that we miss her point. Indeed, immediately after she refrains from troubling the reader with her thoughts, she says, "Though if you look carefully you may find it for yourselves in the course of what I am going to say" (5). In a sense, we have just found it: her point is that women internalize patriarchal strictures against female self-expression.

Through this rhetoric of self-effacement, the narrator also constructs the distinctively female self and style that Woolf celebrates, participating in the strengths of the female tradition as well as its liabilities. She adopts the values of female authorship, rejecting the egotistical "I" of Mr. A and fashioning instead a flexible, fluid "I" that includes several possible identities. When she says, "Call me Mary Beton, Mary Seton, Mary Carmichael or by any name you please—it is not a matter of any importance," she is both the narrator and the characters about whom she writes. This circulation of identities dramatically changes the structure of knowledge in the essay. Here subject and object interpenetrate; in writing about Mary Carmichael the narrator also writes about herself, sharing the stories of all the Marys in her narrative.

The narrator's story is also a kind of self-examination—one that does not exempt her from the frustrations of her subject matter as if she were an Olympian god. Instead it leads to self-knowledge, as when she discovers her anger in the British Museum. Rejecting the role of woman as an aggrandizing mirror of men, the narrator becomes a sympathetic mirror for women, while the writers she discusses reflect her predicament back to her. The image is confirming; it re-visions and clarifies the nature of female experience from the inside, constructing a coherent version of femininity as a counterweight to patriarchal images.

The narrator's cover story operates powerfully through two literary techniques: irony and allusion. Through irony the narrator can encode her insights and attacks while maintaining an air of good humor and equanimity. Let us look at two examples. A simple one is her use of a famous aphorism by Dr. Johnson, that a woman preaching is like a dog's walking on its hind legs: it is not done well, but you are surprised to find it done at all. The narrator imagines Nick Greene, Judith Shakespeare's seducer, saying the same thing about women acting, and quotes a contemporary book about music as saying the same thing about women composing. The narrator counters with her own aphorism: "So accurately does history repeat itself" (54). The point is that history is not history in the sense of an objective record of human experience that repeats itself, because it consists of powerful, quasi-natural forces that cannot be denied. The narrator reduces history to a misogynist joke, repeated over and over.

In another passage the narrator apparently counsels women writers to respectfully tell the truth about men. Because the passage is a rich one, I quote it in full:

> And then I went on very warily, on the tips of my toes (so cowardly am I, so afraid of the lash that was once almost laid on my own shoulders), to murmur that she should also learn to laugh, without bitterness, at the vanities—say rather at the peculiarities, for it is a less offensive word—of the other sex. For there is a spot the size of a shilling at the back of the head which one can never see for oneself. It is one of the good offices that sex can discharge for sex—to describe that spot the size of a shilling at the back of the head. Think how much women have profited by the comments of Juvenal; by the criticism of Strindberg. Think with what humanity and brilliancy men, from the earliest ages, have pointed out to women that dark place at the back of the head! . . . Not of course that any one in their senses would counsel her to hold up to scorn and ridicule of set purpose—literature shows the futility of what is written in that spirit. Be truthful, one would say, and the result is bound to be amazingly interesting. Comedy is bound to be enriched. New facts are bound to be discovered. (90–91)

This passage begins in a very significant way. Once again we see the narrator cowed by authority, this time specified only as "the lash," deliberately revising her comments to avoid punishment and denigrating herself for having done so by calling herself a "coward." She will move cautiously, speak in a "murmer," and, following the advice of the Angel in the House, flatter men if at all possible: the potentially offensive word "vanities" quickly becomes "peculiarities." But while in "Professions for Women" Woolf identified the Angel in the House as the outright enemy of the woman writer, here the narrator finds a way around her, conveying a covert meaning while maintaining a front of politeness. Using the metaphor of the shilling to describe men's lack of self-awareness, she raises the issue of economic power that lies behind her catchphrase "£500 a year." To use the language of money, we might say that men can afford to have blind spots; those exemptions from self-awareness are bought with the shillings and pounds that endow institutions like Oxbridge, where male standards prevail, declaring themselves universal and rendering everything else marginal, distorted, or invisible.

Moreover, when the narrator offers Juvenal and Strindberg as models, she definitely speaks ironically. Juvenal, the Roman poet, is famous for his vitriolic satires of women (his name has come to mean a particularly virulent kind of satire, in contrast to his contemporary, the more indulgent Horace), while Strindberg is probably best known for his misogynist play *Miss Julie*. These male authors succeeded very well in making their reputations with the "scorn and ridicule" that the narrator disingenuously claims is futile. Although the narrator argues that the woman writer should speak "without bitterness," this passage is bitter indeed, although in an encoded way. The contrast between the narrator's cowed murmur and Juvenal's unbuttoned vitriol is implicit but clear. A double standard exists for women's and men's writing, and the narrator feels obliged to follow it because she fears reprisals if she does not. But beneath her ladylike qualifications and the dead-pan prediction of the final sentences—"new facts are bound to be discovered"—lies another moment of buried anger, veiled in quiet sarcasm about the "humanity and brilliancy" with which men have described women. Certainly her own investigations have discovered nothing of the sort.

Woolf's second technique—allusion—also encodes a rich vein of hidden meaning. She names the burial place of Judith Shakespeare as Elephant and Castle, a section of London. This apparently casual, random location in fact contains a whole story, historical rather than fictional, that runs parallel to that of Judith Shakespeare. The name "Elephant and Castle" derives from "Infanta di Castilla" ("Child of Castile," a region of Spain), the name of Catherine of Aragon, the unfortunate first wife of Henry VIII who indirectly caused the establishment of the Anglican Church. By the arrangement of her father,

Catherine had been brought from Spain to marry Henry's older brother, and when he died she was quickly delivered to Henry. The Vatican was summoned to declare that she was still a virgin so that Henry could marry her. Then, after 18 years of marriage during which she did not bear him a son, Henry decided to have the marriage annulled under the pretext that she had not been a virgin at the time of their wedding. Once again the Catholic Church was summoned to pass judgment on Catherine's virginity, but this time the Church balked. Henry staged a trial to "discover" whether Catherine had been a virgin at the time of their marriage but could not force the outcome he desired. In frustration, he broke with the Pope and established the Anglican Church.

Intelligent and talented, Catherine nevertheless followed the only real path open to her—that of a wife. Circulating among men, from father to husband and back again, she is a classic female commodity. Her humiliating dependence on the Church's decision about her virginity reflects the social control over female sexuality. Once again the female body is destiny, the source of vulnerability and oppression. And the translation and corruption of her Spanish name into her husband's language suggests the distortion and suppression of women's voices. Like Judith Shakespeare, she is a woman of great gifts who is not free to exercise them; like her, she is her father's property, to be disposed of in marriage; like her, her body is in the hands of men, inscribed with meanings that are not of her own making. In this complex allusion we see several aspects of Woolf's technique. Here the narrative acts out the predicament of women: Catherine's story is literally submerged beneath the mention of Elephant and Castle. The allusion also contributes to the narrator's cover story; beneath this veiled reference she has concealed her historical knowledge and the indictment of patriarchy it implies. Although Judith Shakespeare might be dismissed as a mere fantasy or "story," as the narrator herself calls it, Catherine's story grounds the fiction of Shakespeare's sister in reality (49).

The close relationship between Judith's and Catherine's experience also continues dismantling the distinction between fact and fiction: we can see the story of Judith Shakespeare grow out of Catherine's experience and can likewise understand Catherine's experience read through the frame of Judith's story as one of archetypal female oppression. From this last observation we might also observe that, as versions of each other, these two women continue the mutuality of identities established through the Marys of the English ballad and through the narrator herself. One could easily proliferate examples of irony and allusion, but the general point remains the same: this apparently rambling, desultory narrative makes some of its most forceful points in covert ways. It does so not only to dramatize the evasions and suppressions of the narrator as a female writer, as I have said, but to illustrate the deftness, complexity, and power of the female style of indirection. The reference to Elephant and Castle is like a trap door in the narrative that discloses a whole world below, enriching the surface with its reinforcing commentary. It may also be a bit of a power play on the part of Virginia Woolf, perhaps a test to weed out readers who are not attuned to her narrator's female sensibility, a sort of code intended only for initiates—that is, for women, whose habits of concealment and suppression make them excellent crackers of codes. These hidden riches, Woolf seems to say, are the fringe benefits of femininity, this secret knowledge a counterweight to the mysteries of Latin and Greek at Oxbridge.

This final observation brings up a question that is also raised by the essay's puzzling narrative structure: Where is Virginia Woolf in all this? Woolf clearly creates the narrator in order to dramatize the nature of female authorship, but why does she shed her own identity so conspicuously? Why not begin and end with the narrator? Instead she bookends the narrator's account with what she represents as her own words, announcing in the final section, "And I will end now in my own person" (105). This "I" is distinct from both the unreal "I" of the narrator and the egotistical "I" of Mr. A. Woolf's conclusion is more factual and less fictional: she quotes the Oxford don Sir Arthur Quiller-Couch on the importance of a university education for a writer, refers to Cambridge rather than Oxbridge, and notes a few key dates in British women's history.

Although Woolf establishes a separate identity in this section, she also joins forces with the narrator. Like the narrator who was chased around Oxbridge, Woolf notes that she has "not been educated at a university" (109) and remarks "I like women," echoing Mary Carmichael's novel in which "Chloe liked Olivia." Recapitulating the narrator's discoveries, Woolf's final "I" puts them to use, as when she offers the narrator's fictional creation of Judith Shakespeare as an inspiration to all women. In that passage, this "I" strengthens her affiliation with the narrator by turning to fiction, saying, "My own suggestion is a little fantastic, I admit" (113). This admission echoes the narrator's self-effacing tone, as her choice of fiction as a way of making her suggestion more acceptable follows the narrator's rhetorical strategy.

In this final section Woolf establishes herself as another version of the unreal "I," perhaps an inheritor of the narrator, adapting those ideas and choices to her own. As an internationally famous writer, Woolf makes a dramatic gesture of modesty and solidarity in identifying herself with the unreal "I" and the several unexalted Marys who populate the essay, embracing the liabilities and values of the female tradition. Looked at in this light, we might regard the final section not as the substitution of Virginia Woolf for her fictional creations but as a ceremony of investiture, in which she takes on their experience as her own.

10

Difficulties and Contradictions: The Blind Spots of *A Room of One's Own*

Thus far I have been taking *A Room of One's Own* at its word, explicating its intentions and presenting it as a coherent, persuasive whole. But the essay does present the reader with certain difficulties. At key points Woolf's thought is in conflict with itself, revealing ambivalence about some of the essay's central issues. It is no insult to suggest that some of the essay's issues remain unresolved or in dispute. To begin with, it is arguably the first feminist literary history, and we could hardly expect it to reflect the feminist thinking that would come after it. While what is often called the second wave of modern feminism, begun in the early 1970s, rescued the essay from obscurity, it has also brought new considerations to bear that Woolf's essay, not surprisingly, did not anticipate. Moreover, many of these issues are thorny ones. The idea of androgyny, for instance, has undergone considerable revision in the last 30 years, going in and out of fashion. The gaps between second-wave feminism and Woolf's essay, along with fluctations in recent feminist thinking, confirm her notion that intellectual and artistic labors are culturally conditioned and historically specific; they change over time as their contexts change. Finally, *A Room of One's*

Own is one of Woolf's first political arguments. She is still in the process of working out and working through difficult issues. It makes sense to regard *A Room of One's Own* as a transitional work in which Woolf begins to divest herself of cultural beliefs about the transcendence of art—traces of which still color her thinking.

The most dramatic problem presented by *A Room of One's Own* is this: despite Woolf's insistence on a gender-specific tradition, she undercuts that notion in several ways. Two comments are widely quoted. One is about Mary Carmichael: "She wrote as a woman, but as a woman who has forgotten that she is a woman, so that her pages were full of that curious sexual quality which comes only when sex is unconscious of itself" (93). What can Woolf mean by this? Why is the path to womanhood unconscious of gender? This is an odd assertion in an argument that takes gender identity so seriously and sees its characteristics as socially constructed. Does Woolf assume that there is an innate femininity lodged in the unconscious that can only be retrieved through forgetfulness? We might wonder, too, what value her own book would have according to this quotation. So much of its purpose is to clarify women's consciousness of their sex and to undo repression. Should the woman writer then forget what she has learned, hoping that her unconscious has somehow assimilated this knowledge and will give it back to her in a more artistic form, without her being aware of it? My questions are meant to suggest how difficult it is to reconcile this passage with the very conscious emphasis on gender in Woolf's essay. Surely no one would imagine that *A Room of One's Own* was written by someone who had forgotten she was a woman.

A second, similar passage occurs toward the end of the essay, its importance underlined by the fact that it is the "very first sentence" that the narrator plans to write on the subject "Women and Fiction": "It is fatal for a woman to lay the least stress on any grievance; to plead even with justice any cause; in any way to speak consciously as a woman. And fatal is no figure of speech; for anything written with that conscious bias is doomed to death" (104). Once again the writer is advised to be unconscious, although perhaps in a more narrow way. In this sentence, to speak consciously as a woman is to express a grievance. Perhaps we can interpret this as a rejection of polemic: Woolf does not want women writers to make speeches in their novels. But her essay often demonstrates the difficulty of *not* laying stress on a grievance and the unhealthy role of repression in maintaining equanimity.

We recall that the narrator avoids a sense of grievance at Oxbridge by internalizing injunctions against women's presence: having been banished from the grass and the library, she has "no wish" to enter the chapel (8). But this lack of desire is a dead end: she has simply acquiesced to patriarchal prohibitions—an act that would hardly free her to write without being conscious of her sex. Throughout much of *A Room of One's Own*, to be a woman is to be aggrieved, and with good reason. How do we judge the works of the women writers Woolf discusses, almost all of whom express anger at their plight? Are they all "doomed to death," unable to "grow in the minds of others" (104), as Woolf claims? Has only Jane Austen survived?

When Woolf introduces "conscious bias" into the passage she further complicates the issue. These terms are not equal; there is a slippage between consciousness of a particular identity, grievance "with justice," and bias. Gender identity, with its distinctive perspective, has degenerated into a distorted perception. Ironically, in this passage Woolf seems guilty of the same kind of misreading that patriarchy has always given women, as when the redoubtable Desmond MacCarthy calls Rebecca West "that arrant feminist" for saying that men are snobs—which Woolf calmly characterizes as "a possibly true if uncomplimentary statement about the other sex" (35). In this kind of misreading, women's protests against male authority are conveniently dismissed as hysterical, distorted, dogmatic, and self-serving. Women's focus on their own experience, including their grievances, is a kind of special pleading, while men's protests against women, in contrast, take on the status of fact. Having deconstructed the notion of objectivity in the British Museum chapter, Woolf seems to reintroduce it in this passage as an appropriate criterion for women's writing.

From these passages it seems clear that Woolf cannot completely divest herself of a belief in the value of transcendence in art even in the face of her more sustained gender-specific and materialist assumptions. In part, Woolf's aesthetic tastes underwrote this contradictory belief.

In the essay "Modern Fiction" she praises the Russian writers as "spiritualists" rather than "materialists" (the label she gave her antagonist Arnold Bennett), because they capture "life or spirit, truth or reality" rather than focusing on the physical and historical details of their stories and characters.[1] According to Woolf, spiritualists reject the depiction of the lives of people as they are embedded in a particular society and focus instead on more abstract philosophical questions: Does life have meaning? What makes us human? Of what does spiritual life consist? In the essay Woolf imagines a kind of primordial state of consciousness that is articulated into lived experience: "The mind receives a myriad of impressions—trivial, fantastic, evanescent, or engraved with the sharpness of steel. From all sides they come, an incessant shower of innumerable atoms; and as they fall, . . . they shape themselves into the life of Monday or Tuesday" (154).

As a novelist, particularly in the period before the publication of *A Room of One's Own*, Woolf obviously attempts to capture the shower of atoms and lets the life of Monday or Tuesday recede into the background—or, rather, she shows the process by which they shape themselves into the particularities of time, place, and individual experience. Woolf's love of the Russian novelists and her own philosophy as expressed here derive from a search for what transcends the here and now.

This viewpoint is clearly at odds with a focus on anything as specific as gender identity as historically constituted. The desire for transcendence runs as an undercurrent throughout *A Room of One's Own*. In her ideal representations of creativity, Woolf frequently uses metaphors of light. When she describes the inspirational effects of the Oxbridge meal, I have said that these metaphors point back to embodied experience. Elsewhere, however, their intangibility suggests a desire to escape from material life. Shakespeare, the ideal artist, is "incandescent" (56); his mind has consumed all impediments to a kind of perfect impersonality, much like that which T. S. Eliot describes in "Tradition and the Individual Talent." The "fire of genius" and the "inner light" that produce and discern great art are also part of the vocabulary of disembodied creativity (72).

Woolf likens the works of "these great artists" to messages written in invisible ink that become clear when held to the light. Somehow they contain what every reader has "felt and known and desired" (72). In place of a distinctive perspective Woolf posits a universal wisdom; in place of the broken sentence and sequence of Mary Carmichael's novel she envisions a kind of ur-truth that is perfectly, wonderfully, and almost mystically intelligible because it is, in some sense, already known, as if it were part of the human genetic code. The narrator's struggles with Mary's novel, her groping attempts to decide whether the novel is original or merely clumsy, drop out of sight. One might argue that Mary's novel has not attained the ideal of great art, otherwise it, too, would evoke this magical response, but Woolf works with an entirely different set of assumptions in these two versions of reading.

The invisibility of the ink suggests the degree to which Woolf's ideal leans toward a disembodied, ahistorical, transcendent version of art, represented as a private, esoteric transaction between writer and reader. On the other hand, Mary Carmichael's authorship, figured in the female rider taking a fence in a crowd of patriarchs, is thoroughly grounded in gender, history, the body, and society. It is not that Mary Carmichael's novel is not as good; it is that Woolf has changed the rules. Thinking of Milton's bogey and of Charles Lamb's incredulity that *Lycidas* was a product of fallible human effort rather than divine inspiration, one wonders whether even the greatest author can blot a line in invisible ink and still work his magic.

With these considerations in mind, it is interesting to return to one example of distorted women's writing—Charlotte Brontë's *Jane Eyre*—because the issue of anger presents another conflict between Woolf's transcendent and materialist beliefs. The narrator criticizes Brontë for allowing her anger to show; because of this slip, her novel is not the incandescent work it ought to be. We might question, however, whether this criticism is too simple, for the narrator's own anger was an important source of insight for her in the British Museum. While Woolf's disappointment with Brontë seems genuine, we should also be alert to the possibility of reading these awkward breaks in a different way. Rather than being only technical flaws, perhaps they are also gateways to a distinctively female point of view. The narrator complains about the "jerk" in the novel when Jane delivers an extended speech about women's need for freedom and hears the laugh that she thinks is the servant Grace Poole's but really belongs to Rochester's mad wife, Bertha, whom he has imprisoned in his house (69). The narrator says that "the continuity is disturbed" by this "awkward break"; Jane's speech has run away with Brontë because it expresses her own grievance about her narrow life, and she must wrest her narrative back on track (69). In constructing this passage Woolf assumes that there is no connection between Jane's speech and the laugh, but, even granting room for the possibility of different interpretations, we might still suggest that Woolf has missed the point of the passage.

In fact, as Sandra Gilbert and Susan Gubar (1979, 349) have argued, the juxtaposition of Jane's speech and Bertha's laugh is thematically crucial; it contrasts the young girl's articulate but naive dreams of freedom with the sardonic and inarticulate yet powerful comment by the incarcerated mad wife, whose place Jane will shortly be asked to take when Rochester proposes. Brontë's "jerk" sharpens the irony of their relationship as both foils and doubles of each other. *Jane Eyre* is very much a cover story, like *A Room of One's Own*, encoding subversive messages about patriarchy and marriage in the figure of the mad wife. It is perhaps unfair to expect Woolf to deliver a particular interpretation of a novel, but it is certainly ironic that Woolf proves her own point with a critical lapse: she has missed the significance of the passage in *Jane Eyre* precisely because Brontë has disturbed the continuity or, to use Woolf's expression, has broken the sequence. Perhaps Woolf was distracted by the vexing issue of anger that the passage from *Jane Eyre* clearly represents, both in Jane's resentment and Bertha's madness. In any case, her insistence on an art free from grievance has led her to misread a now-classic example of women's writing as technically flawed rather than formally and ideologically meaningful.

Woolf's treatment of *Jane Eyre* obliquely and perhaps inadvertently suggests this. Woolf quotes Jane's angry speech at such length that its point commands our attention; in a sense, Woolf turns the stage over to Jane's anger even though she criticizes it. As Mary Jacobus says, this passage "opens up a rift in her own [Woolf's] seamless web. What she herself cannot say without a loss of calmness (rage has been banned in the interests of literature) is uttered instead by another woman writer. The overflow in *Jane Eyre* washes into *A Room of One's Own*."[2] Jacobus implies that Woolf's ambivalence about female anger acts itself out in this passage: She displays Jane's outburst as a covert way of expressing the resentments of the female writer without leaving herself open to charges of personal grievance. As is often the case in this essay, it is difficult to reduce Woolf's "real" point of view to a single attitude. The essay suggests both that Brontë's anger disfigures her writing and that anger is a legitimate, essential source of female self-expression.

This conflict was very much on Woolf's mind as she wrote the essay. On the one hand, writing *A Room of One's Own* was therapeutic for her: "I seem able to write criticism fearlessly. Because of a R. of ones Own I said suddenly to myself last night" (*Diary*, 4: 25). This comment implies that Woolf does not need to disguise her opinions or her emotions. At the same time, the multilayered, allusive narrative also protected Woolf from sensitive material. In a letter to a close friend she writes, "I'm so glad you thought it good tempered—my blood is apt to boil on this one subject . . . and I didn't want it to" (*Letters*, 4: 106). She worried that "if I had said 'Look here, I am uneducated because my brothers used all the family funds'—which is a fact—'Well,' they'd have said, 'she has an axe to grind.'"[3] Woolf explained that she "forced myself to keep my own figure fictitious, legendary," to avoid the charge of personal grievance.[4] Woolf's ceremony of investiture is not entirely symbolic; as a woman writer she shares the conflicts of her narrator.

While Woolf may have legitimate reason to fear expressing anger, her desire to mask her boiling blood beneath a good-tempered facade smacks of the advice of the Angel in the House. The essay's ambiguous use of anger as the source of both artistic blemishes and political insight reflects Woolf's ambivalence about her uncensored self-expression. While Woolf's "I" at the end of the essay has presumably worked through all the issues of the preceding pages, the issue of anger and writing remained unresolved for Virginia Woolf herself. Her sophisticated narrative succeeds perhaps too well in pulling its punches, as contemporary reviews that praise its charm and lightness suggest. Woolf encodes her own anger so completely that it almost disappears, fictionalized and absorbed into the narrator. *A Room of One's Own* can be seen as Woolf's own cover story, distancing her from dangerous material and deflecting her uneasiness as a politicized woman writer into a series of stories about dead and imaginary writers. Given Woolf's fame as a writer, we might regard this phenomenon as a testimony to the power of her insights. If a writer of her stature fears exposure, how might lesser writers feel?

Probably the most controversial aspect of *A Room of One's Own* is its treatment of androgyny—a subject related to the tension between the materialist and transcendent threads in Woolf's argument. Woolf describes an androgynous mind that is more complete and resourceful than a purely masculine or feminine one. While the biological sex determines the dominant gender of the mind, the mind ideally consists of male and female halves. Woolf does not trace out her idea systematically, so it is difficult to tell exactly what she has in mind. Given the unflattering portrait of the masculine mind in her discussion of Kipling, we might wonder what would happen when it meets with its feminine counterpart. Will the mind then be composed of masculinity plus femininity—two self-contained entities that will interact productively with each other? How would such opposites interact except in conflict? Or would each gender dilute the other, so that rather than have "the Flag" on one side of the mind and "Anon" on the other, the androgyne would speak with an assertive but flexible, empathic voice. The generality of Woolf's vision has left the essay subject to reevaluation according to changing perceptions of androgyny. Whether her vision perpetuates the reified gender categories of masculine and feminine or attempts to create a new identity has been at issue since the second wave of feminism recovered the essay in the first place.

Whether the essay is conservative or radical in its formulation of androgyny, the very presence of the idea runs counter to much of Woolf's argument. Having spent so much time and effort constructing a distinctively female style, self, and tradition, she seems to demote such achievements as provisional and imperfect when she promotes a selfhood that goes "beyond" female identity, which is subsumed in the androgynous ideal. Woolf's notion of a single-sex artistic creation as "a horrid little abortion," like her comment that gender consciousness is fatal, flies in the face of her valorization of women's writing (103). One wonders whether Jane Austen, that exemplary inventor of the female sentence, would pass the test of androgyny. Like the passage about the fatality of sex-consciousness, this one is hyperbolic enough to raise a question in the reader's mind about what is at stake. Woolf's strong language seems designed, perhaps unconsciously, to compromise her feminist leanings, to dilute her emphasis on the particularities of gender and creativity. Although the placement of her comments on androgyny toward the end of the book suggests that it represents the culmination of her thinking, it deflects her emphasis on women into a different argument altogether.

Woolf's treatment of androgyny raises other questions as well. In its emphasis on mental faculties, it also erases the body. It disconnects the "nerves that feed the brain" and the gendered body from the imagination, now composed of abstract properties that enter into a mysterious communion (78). Even Judith Shakespeare, prisoner of her body in life, undergoes a sublimation in death, when she is transmuted into a mystical body that women writers bring into being with their achievements. Both Judith Shakespeare's corporeal body and the actual bodies of future women writers disappear beneath the symbolic weight of such a mystical incarnation. It is as if this is the only resolution Woolf can find to the female body's vulnerability, despite her insistence that it forms the foundation of women's authorship. Because of the cultural meanings that are deeply inscribed within it, the body remains an ambiguous source of inspiration. Woolf must insist on its reality, both to retrieve women from Victorian stereotypes of purity and to undo women's oppression. At the same time, however, the body remains haunted by disability and danger, and Woolf longs to escape from its complications. The book's final image, of the woman writer putting on and taking off the body of Judith Shakespeare, figures the essay's vacillation between embodiment and transcendence.

Woolf's construction of androgyny also has the disquieting effect of exalting heterosexual relations. A surprising vision inaugurates the section: a man and a woman enter a taxicab together, prompting the narrator to observe, "One has a profound, if irrational, instinct in favour of the theory that the union of man and woman makes for the greatest satisfaction, the most complete happiness" (98). However one might feel about this instinct in one's own life, it is difficult to reconcile with the unions of men and women that appear in the essay: authoritarian fathers and rebellious daughters; cavalier theater managers and their pregnant, despairing mistresses; selfish kings and their discarded—if not beheaded—wives. The language of the androgyny passage relies heavily on metaphors of sexuality, childbirth, and marriage—hardly instances of female happiness throughout the essay. In the face of the image that comes to the narrator's mind in the previous chapter—that of a middle-aged woman and her elderly mother—it is disappointingly conventional in terms of both narrative and politics. We are back to "boy meets girl." The image is also conventional in relation to the subtext of lesbianism. One wonders how Woolf's writing of *Orlando*, inspired by her lover Vita Sackville-West, or the writing she did with Sackville-West's advice and encouragement could find a place in this theory of creativity.

Above the conflicts and inequities of the real world, the androgynous mind withdraws to "celebrate its nuptials in darkness" (104). Woolf imagines this mental life as magically exempt from patriarchy, a consummation of the taxicab scene and the narrator's belief that, despite its part in the oppression of women, heterosexuality is best after all. Perhaps, like the mystical body of Judith Shakespeare, these nighttime nuptials represent an attempted resolution as well as a contradiction, transposing heterosexuality into an abstract and imaginative power in order to rescue it from its dangerous, even fatal, consequences for women. It may also be exactly what Woolf says it is: "a profound if irrational" investment in the very social structures she sets out to criticize, reminding us how difficult it is to think of one's self out of one's culture.

Critics have raised two other signficant objections to *A Room of One's Own*, both of which reflect changing ideas in contemporary literary criticism. First, it has been argued that Woolf's depiction of a female literary tradition is inaccurate and incomplete. No one could fault Woolf for not knowing about women authors and varieties of female experience that were unknown in her age, of course. The problem is that Woolf's essay has been so influential that it has shaped modern accounts of women's writing even in the face of contradictory evidence. Woolf tells a story of women's literature that consists of little but silence and suffering through the Renaissance; that barely begins until the eighteenth century, with Aphra Behn; and that posits an evolution in women's writing that depends in part on very specific criteria, such as commercial publication, the use of particular genres such as the novel, and public success.

According to Margaret Ezell, these assumptions are difficult to maintain in the light of modern scholarship.[5] For one thing, efforts to recover women writers before the eighteenth century have succeeded beyond Woolf's imagination, although contemporary collections such as *The Norton Anthology of Literature by Women* continue to regard earlier periods as relative wastelands of women's literature.[6] For another, Ezell argues, earlier women writers were prolific practitioners of forms such as religious essays, advice books, and prophetic writings, along with the diaries and letters that Woolf acknowledges, and that these forms had more prestige in their era than in ours. Imposing twentieth-century notions of which genres "count" is anachronistic. And even if these kinds of writing never enjoyed the status of the epic poem, we might still question the wisdom of applying a traditional hierarchy of importance to women's writing given Woolf's emphasis on difference. To judge it by the same standards is to misread it.

Woolf's essays on traditionally "minor" women authors as well as *A Room of One's Own* betray an allegiance to conventional standards, even as they set out to revise them. Woolf's ambivalence about figures such as the Duchess of Newcastle or Lady Winchilsea suggests that, while she wishes to acknowledge female achievement wherever it appears, she remains uneasy about promoting work that has traditionally been considered second-rate. As one critic says, "Woolf's own excavations [of forgotten women writers] were marked by a cultural wariness of and palpable disdain for 'minor' literary achievements."[7]

Moreover, Ezell, argues, many women writers of the Renaissance wrote poetry for circulation among a coterie of intellectuals and not for publication as we know it, just as their male counterparts did. In such circles manuscripts, not publications, are the index of achievement. Because Woolf focused on writing as a means of economic empowerment, she may have been less open to the value of other, less professionalized contexts for writing. She may also have underestimated the extent to which these women participated in literary culture. Judith Shakespeare may not be entirely representative of women writers in the Renaissance, isolated and silenced. Ironically, according to Ezell, because *A Room of One's Own* has achieved such fame, it has carried more authority than it deserves in shaping our modern understanding of women's writing in the past.

Finally, and extremely important, is the critique that women of color have made of Woolf. Woolf's inspiring model of a coherent, collective female voice, symbolized by Judith Shakespeare, has also effaced difference. Once again the point is not to blame Woolf for her failure to anticipate changes in modern feminist criticism but to note the ways in which the blind spots of this influential essay have moved others to continue its project of re-vision. Woolf herself may have been a powerful foremother for some writers, but her economic, class, and racial privilege make her a problematic ancestor for writers of different backgrounds. Woolf's critique of Empire has not erased all traces of racism, for example. When she praises women for not wishing to make an Englishwoman out of a "very fine negress," she implies that her reader is white and the Negress remains other—perhaps already commodified by the adjective "fine," often applied to the accoutrements of expensive living, such as fine wine and fine china.[8] While Woolf's woman writer might not want to colonize the black woman, neither does she identity with her. The flexible selfhood of women writers does not, apparently, extend to other races.

The African-American writer Alice Walker, author of *The Color Purple*, addresses this difficulty in her famous essay "In Search of Our Mothers' Gardens." In many ways Walker's essay deliberately parallels Woolf's. Walker also seeks female creativity in unusual places in order to connect her artistic aspirations with the past. Like Woolf, Walker reevaluates forgotten women, including her own mother, whose gardens were the envy of everyone who saw them. Walker quotes *A Room of One's Own* directly, showing her sense of inheritance from Woolf as a woman writer and historian of creativity. At the same time, however, she revises Woolf's text by inserting her own race-specific additions. Considering the case of Phillis Wheatley, the eighteenth-century African-American poet, she writes,

> Virginia Woolf wrote further, speaking of course not of our Phillis, that "any woman born with a great gift in the sixteenth century [insert "eighteenth-century," insert "black woman," insert "born or made a slave"] would certainly have gone crazed. . . . For it needs little skill and psychology to be sure that a highly gifted girl who had tried to use her gift for poetry would have been so thwarted and hindered by contrary instincts [add "chains, guns, the lash, ownership of one's body by someone else, submission to an alien religion"], that she must have lost her health and sanity to a certainty."[9]

With these insertions, Walker tells the story of the African-American woman writer, whose experience in slavery intensifies and alters the dynamics of oppression and repression that Woolf describes. There will be both common ground and divergence in the experiences of black and white women writers. Woolf argues that male standards have masqueraded as universal ones and that they leave out the story of women writers. Walker says that the standards of white women have masqueraded as universal ones for women, absorbing or marginalizing the works of African-American women just as British patriarchy silences women. Ironically, we find Virginia Woolf in the position of Arthur Quiller-Couch, arguing for an expanded understanding of the material conditions of creativity but leaving out a significant set of voices and experiences because of her own blind spot.

Thus while Woolf's essay has been deeply influential and is frequently cited as a classic text of feminist thought, it continues to inspire discussion and controversy. The essay's fame makes it worth fighting over, and with. It remains a text to be reckoned with, whatever its contradictions and blind spots. In many ways *A Room of One's Own* has set the agenda for modern feminist criticism. Therefore it is continually renewed, not by some mystical force that annoints masterpieces but by the sustained interest its historical significance provokes for women, and men, who enter the conversation from their own points of view and social positions.

Notes and References

1. Virginia Woolf and Her World

1. "A Sketch of the Past," in *Moments of Being*, 2d ed., ed. Jeanne Schulkind (New York: Harcourt, Brace, Jovanovich, 1985), 150.

2. "22 Hyde Park Gate," in *Moments of Being*, 174.

3. "Old Bloomsbury," in *Moments of Being*, 192; hereafter cited in text.

4. Duncan Grant, *Horizon* 3, no. 18 (June 1941): 405; quoted in Phyllis Rose, *Woman of Letters: A Life of Virginia Woolf* (Oxford: Oxford University Press, 1978), 39.

5. Ray Strachey, *The Cause: A Short History of the Women's Movement in Britain* (1978), quoted in Susan Kingsley Kent, *Sex and Suffrage in Britain, 1860–1914* (Princeton: Princeton University Press, 1987), 197.

6. Sandra Gilbert and Susan Gubar, *No Man's Land: The Place of the Woman Writer in the Twentieth Century*, vol. 1, *The War of the Words* (New Haven: Yale University Press, 1988), 36.

7. *The Letters of Virginia Woolf*, vol. 2, 1912–22, ed. Nigel Nicolson and Joanne Trautmann (New York: Harcourt, Brace, Jovanovich, 1976), 76; hereafter cited in text.

2. The Importance of *A Room of One's Own*

1. *The Letters of Virginia Woolf*, vol. 4, 1929–31, ed. Nigel Nicolson and Joanne Trautmann (New York: Harcourt, Brace, Jovanovich, 1978), 102; hereafter cited in text.

2. Margaret Drabble, *Virginia Woolf: A Personal Debt* ([New York]: Aloe Editions, 1973), 3; quoted in Alex Zwerdling, *Virginia Woolf and the Real World* (Berkeley and Los Angeles: University of California Press, 1986), 211.

3. Jane Marcus, "Thinking Back through Our Mothers," *New Feminist Essays on Virginia Woolf*, ed. Jane Marcus (Lincoln: University of Nebraska Press, 1981), 1.

4. Louise DeSalvo, *Virginia Woolf: The Impact of Childhood Sexual Abuse on Her Life and Work* (Boston: Beacon Press, 1989).

3. Critical Reception

1. *The Diary of Virginia Woolf*, vol. 3, 1925–30, ed. Anne Olivier Bell (assisted by Andrew McNeillie) (New York: Harcourt, Brace, Jovanovich, 1980), 17; hereafter cited in text.

2. N. Elizabeth Monroe, "The Inception of Mrs. Woolf's Art," *College English* 2 (1940): 228.

3. Orlo Williams, "Books of the Quarter" (review of the *Uniform Edition of the Works of Virginia Woolf* and *A Room of One's Own*), *Criterion: A Literary Review* 9 (1930): 509; hereafter cited in text.

4. Arnold Bennett, "Queen of the High-Brows," *Evening Standard*, 28 November 1929, 9.

5. *Times of London Literary Supplement*, 31 October 1929, 867; hereafter cited in text.

6. *New York Times Book Review*, 10 November 1929, 2; hereafter cited in text.

7. *New York Herald-Tribune Literary Supplement*, 27 October, 1929, 1; hereafter cited in text.

8. Aileen D. Lorberg, "Virginia Woolf, Benevolent Satirist," *Personality* 33 (1952): 150; hereafter cited in text.

9. Elisabeth Woodbridge, "Speaking for Women," *Yale Review* 19 (1929): 628; hereafter cited in text.

10. *New York World*, 29 October 1929, 15; hereafter cited in text.

11. *Springfield Republican*, 26 December 1929, 6.

12. Angus Wilson, "The Always-Changing Impact of Virginia Woolf," *British Novelists since 1900*, ed. Jack Biles (New York: AMS Press, 1987), 69.

13. E. M. Forster, "Virginia Woolf," in *Two Cheers for Democracy* (New York: Harcourt, Brace, Jovanovich, 1951), 255.

14. Brenda Silver, "The Authority of Anger: *Three Guineas* as Case Study," *Signs: Journal of Women in Culture and Society* 16 (1991): 341.

15. Jane Marcus, "Storming the Toolshed," *Signs: Journal of Women in Culture and Society* 7 (1982): 622–40.

16. Elaine Showalter, *A Literature of Their Own: British Women Novelists from Brontë to Lessing* (Princeton: Princeton University Press, 1977), 282.

17. Rachel Bowlby, *Virginia Woolf: Feminist Destinations* (London: Basil Blackwell, 1988).

4. Women's Colleges and *A Room of One's Own*

1. *Women and Fiction: The Manuscript Versions of A Room of One's Own*, ed. S. P. Rosenbaum (London: Basil Blackwell, 1992), xv–xvi; hereafter cited in text.

2. Rita McWilliams-Tullberg, "Women and Degrees at Cambridge University, 1862–1897," in *A Widening Sphere: Changing Roles of Victorian Women*, ed. Martha Vicinus (Bloomington: Indiana University Press, 1977), 136.

3. Quoted in Perry Williams, "Pioneer Women Students at Cambridge," *Lessons for Life: The Schooling of Girls and Women, 1850–1950*, ed. Felicity Hunt (London: Basil Blackwell, 1987), 190.

4. "Professions for Women," in *The Death of the Moth and Other Essays* (1942; New York: Harcourt, Brace, Jovanovich, 1970), 237; hereafter cited in text.

5. Women and Society: Patriarchy and the Place of the Outsider

1. It is difficult to determine the equivalent of this sum in modern American dollars, as British currency has been revalued since Woolf's essay was published and equivalence does not give a sense of the buying power or standard of living that £500 could command. It is safe to say that it represents a living somewhere between subsistence and comfort. One 1929 review assesses it as about $2,000, or the equivalent of a Guggenheim Fellowship, saying, "It does not seem so very difficult for the sex to get" (*New York World*, 15). In 1992–93 the Guggenheim Foundation awarded an average grant of $26,500, a significant although not a princely sum. It might be more helpful to compare Woolf's actual writing income with this fictional standard. In 1929 she anticipated making £30 a month for her essays, or £360 a year (*Diary*, 3: 175); this represents only a portion of her income. In 1920 she reported earning £2,000 from the sales of *Orlando* (*Diary*, 3: 232). *A Room of One's Own* sold even better, providing an entire year's income (*Diary*, 3: 272–73). Although the Woolfs did not live extravagantly, they lived in relative comfort, enjoying a rich social life and regular trips abroad. It is interesting to note that, in 1929, the net income of the Hogarth Press, owned and run by Virginia and Leonard Woolf, was £580; the director's annual salary was £700 (J. H. Willis, Jr., *Leonard and Virginia Woolf as Publishers: The Hogarth Press, 1917–1941* [Charlottesville: University of Virginia Press, 1992], Appendix B [406].)

2. *The Letters of Virginia Woolf*, vol. 1, 1882–1912, ed. Nigel Nicolson and Joanne Trautmann (New York: Harcourt, Brace, Jovanovich, 1975), 45; hereafter cited in text.

3. *The Diary of Virginia Woolf*, vol. 4, 1931–35, ed. Anne Olivier Bell

(assisted by Andrew McNeillie) (New York: Harcourt, Brace, Jovanovich, 1982), 35; hereafter cited in text.

4. *The Diary of Virginia Woolf*, vol. 2, 1920–24, ed. Anne Olivier Bell (assisted by Andrew McNeillie) (New York: Harcourt, Brace, Jovanovich, 1978), 339; hereafter cited in text.

5. *Three Guineas* (1938; New York: Harcourt, Brace, Jovanovich, 1966), 101; hereafter cited in text.

6. "Mr. Bennett and Mrs. Brown," in *The Death of the Moth*, 96; hereafter cited in text.

7. "The New Biography," in *Granite and Rainbow* (New York: Harcourt, Brace, Jovanovich, 1970), 149.

8. Adrienne Rich, "When We Dead Awaken: Writing as Re-Vision," in *Adrienne Rich's Poetry and Prose*, ed. Barbara Charlesworth Gelpi and Albert Gelpi (1975; New York: W. W. Norton, 1993), 167–68; hereafter cited in text.

9. *Jacob's Room* (1922; New York: Harcourt, Brace, Jovanovich, 1950), 32.

10. Marcia McClintock Folsom, "Gallant Red Brick and Plain China: Teaching *A Room of One's Own*," *College English* 45 (1983): 255; hereafter cited in text.

11. *The Letters of Virginia Woolf*, vol. 5, 1936–41, ed. Nigel Nicolson and Joanne Trautmann (New York: Harcourt, Brace, Jovanovich, 1984), 34–35; hereafter cited in text.

12. Patrick McGee, "Woolf's Other: The University in Her Eye," *Novel: A Forum on Fiction* 23 (1990): 236.

13. Jane Marcus, "'Taking the Bull by the Udders': Sexual Difference in Virginia Woolf—a Conspiracy Theory," in *Virginia Woolf and the Languages of Patriarchy* (Bloomington: Indiana University Press, 1987), 145.

6. A Sociology of Creativity

1. T. S. Eliot, "Tradition and the Individual Talent," in *Selected Essays* (1932; New York: Harcourt, Brace, Jovanovich, 1964), 7.

2. Quoted by John Halperin, "Jane Austen's Nineteenth-Century Criticism," in *Jane Austen: Bicentenary Essays*, ed. John Halperin (Cambridge: Cambridge University Press, 1975), 23, from *The Letters of Edward Fitzgerald*, vol. 2 (London, 1894), 131.

7. Social Institutions and Creativity

1. Pierre Bourdieu, *Distinction: A Social Critique of the Judgment of Taste*, trans. Richard Nice (1979; Cambridge: Harvard University Press, 1984), 7.

2. Damian Riehl Leader, *A History of the University of Cambridge*, vol. 1, *The University of 1546* (Cambridge: Cambridge University Press, 1988), 23.

3. Dr. Henry Maudsley, "Sex and Mind in Education," *Fortnightly Review*, April 1874, quoted in *Strong-Minded Women and Other Lost Voices from Nineteenth-Century England*, ed. Janet Horowitz Murray (New York: Pantheon Books, 1982), 221.

4. Joan N. Burstyn, *Victorian Education and the Ideal of Womanhood* (1980; New Brunswick: Rutgers University Press, 1984), 37.

5. Michel Foucault, *Power/Knowledge: Selected Interviews and Other Writings, 1972–1977*, ed. and trans. Colin Gordon (New York: Pantheon, 1980), 234.

8. Female Creativity and Literary History

1. Charlotte Brontë, "Biographical Notice of Ellis and Acton Bell," in *Wuthering Heights* (New York: W. W. Norton, 1990), 315.

2. Jane Marcus, "Liberty, Sorority, Misogyny," in *Virginia Woolf and the Languages of Patriarchy*, 87.

3. *Jane Austen's Letters to Her Sister Cassandra and Others*, 2d ed., ed. R. W. Chapman (London: Oxford University Press, 1952), 401, quoted in Sandra Gilbert and Susan Gubar, *The Madwoman in the Attic: The Woman Writer and the Nineteenth-Century Literary Imagination* (New Haven: Yale University Press, 1979), 109; hereafter cited in text.

4. W. H. Auden, "Letter to Lord Byron," in *Collected Poems*, ed. Edward Mendelson (New York: Random House, 1978), 29.

5. "Romance and the Heart," in *Contemporary Writers* (New York: Harcourt, Brace, Jovanovich, 1965), 124–25.

6. Hélène Cixous, "The Laugh of the Medusa," trans. Keith Cohen and Paula Cohen, *Signs: Journal of Women in Culture and Society* 1 (1976): 881.

7. Jane Marcus, "Sapphistry: Narration as Lesbian Seduction," in *Virginia Woolf and the Languages of Patriarchy*, 175; hereafter cited in text.

8. Gayle Rubin, "The Traffic in Women: Notes on the 'Political Economy' of Sex," in *Toward an Anthropology of Women*, ed. Rayna Rapp Reiter (New York: Monthly Review Press, 1975), 177.

9. Luce Irigaray, *This Sex Which Is Not One*, trans. Catherine Porter (1977; Ithaca, N.Y.: Cornell University Press, 1985), 196.

10. Difficulties and Contradictions: The Blinds Spots of *A Room of One's Own*

1. "Modern Fiction," in *The Common Reader* (1925; New York: Harcourt, Brace, Jovanovich, 1953), 153; hereafter cited in text.

2. Mary Jacobus, *Reading Women: Essays in Feminist Criticism* (New York: Columbia University Press, 1986), 35.

3. Christopher St. John, *Ethyl Smyth* (London: Longmans Green, 1959), 229, 230; quoted in Jane Marcus, *Art and Anger: Reading Like a Woman* (Columbus: Ohio State University Press, 1988), 112–13.

4. Jane Marcus, "'No More Horses,'" in *Art and Anger*, 113.

5. Margaret J. M. Ezell, "The Myth of Judith Shakespeare: Creating the Canon of Women's Literature," *New Literary History: A Journal of Theory and Interpretation* 21 (1990): 579–92.

6. *The Norton Anthology of Literature by Women: The Tradition in English*, ed. Sandra Gilbert and Susan Gubar (New York: W. W. Norton, 1985).

7. Bradford K. Mudge, "Burning Down the House: Sara Coleridge, Virginia Woolf, and the Politics of Literary Revision," *Tulsa Studies in Women's Literature* 5 (1986): 231.

8. Elizabeth Abel, "Matrilineage and the Racial 'Other': Woolf and Her Literary Daughters of the Second Wave," paper read at the Third Annual Virginia Woolf Conference, Jefferson City, Mo., 13 June 1993.

9. Alice Walker, "In Search of Our Mothers' Gardens," in *In Search of Our Mothers' Gardens* (New York: Harcourt, Brace, Jovanovich, 1983), 235; my ellipses.

Selected Bibliography

Primary Works

The Voyage Out. 1915. New York: Harcourt, Brace, Jovanovich, 1948.

Jacob's Room. 1922. New York: Harcourt, Brace, Jovanovich, 1950.

Mrs. Dalloway. 1925. New York: Harcourt, Brace, Jovanovich, 1953.

The Common Reader. 1925. New York: Harcourt, Brace, Jovanovich, 1953.

To the Lighthouse. 1927. New York: Harcourt, Brace, Jovanovich, 1954.

Orlando. 1928. New York: Harcourt, Brace, Jovanovich, 1956.

A Room of One's Own. 1929. New York: Harcourt, Brace, Jovanovich, 1957, 1981. Introduction by Mary Gordon.

The Years. 1937. New York: Harcourt, Brace, Jovanovich, 1966.

Three Guineas. 1938. New York: Harcourt, Brace, Jovanovich, 1965.

The Death of the Moth and Other Essays. 1942. New York: Harcourt, Brace, Jovanovich, 1970.

The Captain's Death Bed and Other Essays. 1950. New York: Harcourt, Brace, Jovanovich, 1970.

Granite and Rainbow. 1958. New York: Harcourt, Brace, Jovanovich, 1970.

Contemporary Writers. New York: Harcourt, Brace, Jovanovich, 1965.

The Collected Essays of Virginia Woolf. 4 vols. Edited Leonard Woolf. New York: Harcourt, Brace, Jovanovich, 1967.

The Diary of Virginia Woolf. 5 vols. Edited by Anne Olivier Bell. New York: Harcourt, Brace, Jovanovich, 1977–84.

The Letters of Virginia Woolf. 6 vols. Edited by Nigel Nicolson and Joanne Trautmann. New York: Harcourt, Brace, Jovanovich, 1975–80.

Moments of Being. 2d ed. Edited by Jeanne Schulkind. New York: Harcourt, Brace, Jovanovich, 1985.

Women and Fiction: The Manuscript Versions of "A Room of One's Own." Transcribed and edited by S. P. Rosenbaum. London: Basil Blackwell, 1992.

Secondary Works

Books

Abel, Elizabeth. *Virginia Woolf and the Fictions of Psychoanalysis.* Chicago: University of Chicago Press, 1989.

Bazin, Nancy T. *Virginia Woolf and the Androgynous Vision.* New Brunswick: Rutgers University Press, 1973. Early, sympathetic exploration of idea of androgyny in Woolf's fiction, including *A Room of One's Own.*

Bell, Quentin. *Virginia Woolf: A Biography.* 2 vols. New York: Harcourt, Brace, Jovanovich, 1972. The most complete and detailed Woolf biography, written by her nephew. Challenged by feminist scholars because of its portrait of Woolf as fragile and apolitical.

Bowlby, Rachel. *Virginia Woolf: Feminist Destinations.* New York: Basil Blackwell, 1988. Emphasis on Woolf's feminist thought as exploratory and multifaceted. Treats most of the novels and *A Room of One's Own.*

DeSalvo, Louise. *Virginia Woolf: The Impact of Childhood Sexual Abuse on Her Life and Work.* Boston: Beacon Press, 1989. Provocative although sometimes unconvincing study.

DiBattista, Maria. *Virginia Woolf's Major Novels: The Fables of Anon.* New Haven: Yale University Press, 1980. Discusses the idea of anonymity as characterizing Woolf's theory of narrative; addresses the major novels.

Majumdar, Robin, and Allen McLauren, eds. *Virginia Woolf: The Critical Heritage.* London: Routledge, 1975. Selections from reviews of Woolf's works.

Marcus, Jane. *Art and Anger: Reading like a Woman.* Columbus: Ohio State University Press, 1988. Provocative essays on Woolf's feminist thought, with frequent reference to *A Room of One's Own* and the politics of Woolf criticism.

_____ . *Virginia Woolf and the Languages of Patriarchy.* Bloomington: Indiana University Press, 1987. More provocative essays, including several devoted to *A Room of One's Own.*

Marder, Herbet. *Virginia Woolf: Feminism and Art.* Chicago: University of Chicago Press, 1968. Probably the first attempt to address Woolf's feminist thought; includes extensive reference to *A Room of One's Own.*

Bibliography

Rose, Phyllis. *Woman of Letters: A Life of Virginia Woolf*. New York: Oxford University Press, 1978. Biography focusing on Woolf as woman writer, paying attention to her memoirs and major novels.

Rosenman, Ellen Bayuk. *The Invisible Presence: Virginia Woolf and the Mother-Daughter Relationship*. Baton Rouge: Louisiana State University Press, 1986. Study of Woolf's female aesthetic, including a chapter on female literary history.

Showalter, Elaine. *A Literature of Their Own: British Women Novelists from Brontë to Lessing*. Princeton: Princeton University Press, 1977. A literary history of women writers; includes a well-known attack on Woolf's interest of androgyny as an escape from feminism.

Zwerdling, Alex. *Virginia Woolf and the Real World*. Berkeley: University of California, 1986. Study of Woolf's political thought, including feminism.

Articles and Book Chapters

Black, Naomi. "Virginia Woolf and the Women's Movement." In *Virginia Woolf: A Feminist Slant*, edited by Jane Marcus, 180–97. Lincoln: University of Nebraska Press, 1983. Details Woolf's participation in feminist organizations.

Ezell, Margaret J. M. "The Myth of Judith Shakespeare: Creating the Canon of Women's Literature." *New Literary History* 21 (1990): 579–92. Excellent discussion of how *A Room of One's Own* has distorted modern female literary history.

Farwell, Marilyn R. "Virginia Woolf and Androgyny." *Contemporary Literature* 16 (1975): 433–51. Special emphasis on *A Room of One's Own*.

Folsom, Marcia McClintock. "Gallant Red Brick and Plain China: Teaching *A Room of One's Own*." *College English* 45 (1983): 254–62. Emphasis on how to stimulate discussion about the essay in the classroom, especially on handling students' difficulties and resistance.

Froula, Christine. "Virginia Woolf as Shakespeare's Sister: Chapters in a Women Writer's Autobiography." In *Women's Re-Visions of Shakespeare: On the Responses of Dickinson, Woolf, Rich, H.D., George Eliot, and Others*, edited by Marianne Novy, 123–42. Urbana: University of Illinois Press, 1990. Explores Woolf's investment in the idea of a female Shakespeare.

Gilbert, Sandra M., and Susan Gubar. *No Man's Land: The Place of the Woman Writer in the Twentieth Century*. Vol. 1, *The War of the Words*. New Haven: Yale University Press, 1988. Includes chapter "Sexual Linguistics: Women's Sentence, Man's Sentencing," which contrasts male and female writers' fantasies about language, with extensive references to Woolf's female aesthetic in *A Room of One's Own*.

Jacobus, Mary. *Reading Women: Essays in Feminist Criticism*. New York: Columbia University Press, 1986. Includes chapter "The Difference in View," with excellent discussion of Woolf's conception of sexual difference, particularly as it is inscribed in language.

Jones, Ellen Carol. "Androgynous Vision and Artistic Process in Virginia Woolf's *A Room of One's Own*." In *Critical Essays on Virginia Woolf*, edited by Morris Beja, 227–39. Boston: G. K. Hall, 1985. Exploration of the complexities of androgyny.

Klein, Kathleen Gregory. "A Common Sitting Room: Virginia Woolf's Critique of Women Writers." In *Virginia Woolf: Centenary Essays*, edited by Elaine K. Ginsberg and Laura Moss Gottlieb. Troy, N.Y.: Whitson Publishing, 1983. Discussion of the politics of space in Woolf's essays on women writers.

McGee, Patrick. "Woolf's Other: The University in Her Eye." *Novel: A Forum on Fiction* 23 (1990): 229–46. Examination of Woolf's understanding of the university as a patriarchal institution and her resistance to its habits and values.

Modern Fiction Studies 38 (1992). Special issue on Virginia Woolf. Includes nearly comprehensive bibliography, 1972–92 (excluding dissertations and articles of fewer than five pages).

Moi, Toril. *Sexual/Textual Politics: Feminist Literary Theory*. London: Methuen, 1986. Includes chapter "Introduction: Who's Afraid of Virginia Woolf" that discusses feminist critics' use and misuse of *A Room of One's Own*.

Mudge, Bradford. "Burning Down the House: Sara Coleridge, Virginia Woolf, and the Politics of Literary Revision." *Tulsa Studies in Women's Literature* 5 (1986): 229–50. Treats *A Room of One's Own* peripherally but nevertheless offers important insight into Woolf's ambivalence about recovering "minor" women writers.

Rigney, Barbara Hill. "'A Wreath upon the Grave': The Influence of Virginia Woolf on Feminist Critical Theory." In *Criticism and Critical Theory*, edited by Jeremy Hawthorn, 72–81. London: Arnold, 1984. Discussion of the manifold ways in which Woolf's thought has been appropriated by modern feminist criticism.

Rosenman, Ellen Bayuk. "Sexual Identity and *A Room of One's Own*: 'Secret Economies' in Virginia Woolf's Feminist Discourse." *Signs: Journal of Women in Culture and Society* 14 (1989): 634–50. Discussion of the meaning of lesbianism in the 1920s, including its relationship to feminism and androgyny.

Bibliography

Silver, Brenda. "What's Woolf Got to Do with It? Or, The Perils of Popularity." *Modern Fiction Studies* 38 (1992): 21–60. Witty exploration of Woolf's status and meaning as cultural icon.

Squier, Susan. "Mirroring and Mothering: Reflections on the Mirror Encounter Metaphor in Virginia Woolf's Works." *Twentieth Century Literature* 27 (1980): 272–88. Contrasts different kinds of mirroring in Woolf's work, including the aggrandizing reflection of men by women discussed in *A Room of One's Own*.

Walker, Alice. "In Search of Our Mothers' Gardens." In *In Search of Our Mothers' Gardens*. New York: Harcourt, Brace, Jovanovich, 1983. Theory of African-American creativity that appropriates and revises *A Room of One's Own*.

Index

A., Mr., 52, 84, 91, 93, 97, 101
allusion, 97, 99–101
androgyny, 13, 104, 110–12
Angel in the House, 24, 36, 67, 82, 98, 109
anger, 15, 20, 67, 75, 97, 108–9
anonymity, 23, 47, 73, 81–82, 84, 89, 94, 95–96, 110
The Apostles (Cambridge Conversazione Society), 58
Auden, W. H., 18, 43; "Letter to Lord Byron," 78
Austen, Jane, 33, 35, 39, 47, 51, 52, 72, 75, 77, 78, 89, 105

Balzac, Honoré de, 79
Beerbohm, Max, 60
Behn, Aphra, 35
Bell, Clive, 58
Bennett, Arnold, 15, 17, 32, 33, 106; *Our Women*, 32
Beowulf, 63
Beton, Mary, 34, 81, 89, 90, 92, 95

Biron, Sir Charles, 88, 89
Bloomsbury, 5, 6, 18, 19, 32, 57
Borges, Jorge Luis, 91
Botticelli, Sandro: *The Birth of Venus*, 61
Bourdieu, Pierre, 54, 57
British Museum, 42, 48, 54, 55, 63, 64, 66, 73, 70, 76, 92, 97, 105
Brontë, Charlotte, 34, 35, 39, 51, 72–73, 75, 107; *Jane Eyre*, 75, 107–9
Brontë, Emily, 35, 39, 51, 72–73
Browning, Oscar, 52
Burne-Jones, Edward, 3

Cambridge University, 5, 22, 23, 31, 32, 41, 54
Cameron, Julia Margaret, 3
Carmichael, Mary, in *A Room of One's Own*, 24, 81, 86, 89, 90, 93, 95, 104, 107; author of *Love's Creation*, 86
Case, Janet, 8

Index

Hitler, Adolph, 18
Hogarth Press, 6, 31
Horace, 99

ideology, 7, 19, 30, 33, 38, 40, 50, 70
imperialism, 20, 34, 46, 83, 90, 110, 114
Infant Custody Act, 50
Irigaray, Luce, 88
irony, 17, 44, 97, 98
Isherwood, Christopher, 18

Jacob's Room, 6, 15, 41
James, Henry, 3, 5, 9
Johnson, Samuel, 97
Joyce, James, 19; *Dubliners*, 6; *Ulysses*, 6
Juvenal, 98–99

Keynes, John Maynard, 9
Kipling, Rudyard, 48, 83, 91

Lamb, Charles, 60, 70, 71, 107
Lawrence, D. H., *The Rainbow*, 6
lesbianism, 6, 20, 88, 89, 112
Lessing, Doris, 11
Lewes, George Henry, 51
Life and Letters, 33
London Library Committee, 31

MacCarthy, Desmond, 32–33, 44, 46, 49, 52
McGee, Patrick, 45
Magna Carta, 63
Mansfield, Katherine, 35
Marcus, Jane, 45, 73, 88
marginalization, 13, 42, 44, 45, 64, 84
Married Women's Property Act, 49, 50
masculinity, 4–5, 11, 16, 36, 41, 56, 67, 89

masterpieces, 12, 14, 29
Maudsley, Dr. Henry, 56
Meredith, George, 4
Milton, John, 71–72, 84, 107; *Lycidas*, 60, 71; *Paradise Lost*, 71–72
"Modern Fiction," 106
modernism, 6, 8–9, 14, 15, 32; stream-of-consciousness technique, 7, 15, 18, 37, 78, 83
mothers, 13, 43, 49, 50, 72, 78, 85–86
"Mr. Bennett and Mrs. Brown," 32, 36
Mrs. Dalloway, 11, 31, 35, 36, 61, 78, 89

Naremore, James, *The World without a Self*, 82
narrator, 23, 30, 31, 34, 41, 44, 45, 58, 61, 67, 68, 69, 70, 77, 86, 92, 94–95, 100, 101
Nation and Athenaeum, 88
New York Times Book Review, 17, 47, 51

Onerva, 11
Orlando, 5, 89, 112
Osborne, Dorothy, 70, 73, 82, 86, 94
Oxbridge, 23, 39, 41, 42, 43, 51, 52, 55, 58, 60, 63
Oxford University, 23, 30, 54, 56

Pankhurst, Christabel, 7
Pankhurst, Emmeline, 7
patriarchy, 3–5, 12, 23, 30, 33, 34, 38, 42, 46, 54, 70, 115
Plato, 4, 5
Pope, Alexander, 48
Post-Impressionist Exhibition, 58
"Professions for Women," 24, 35, 36, 37, 98

The Author

Ellen Bayuk Rosenman is an associate professor of English and a member of the Women's Studies Program at the University of Kentucky. She is the author of *The Invisible Presence: Virginia Woolf and the Mother-Daughter Relationship* (1986), as well as articles on Virginia Woolf, George Eliot, Charlotte Brontë, and Elizabeth Gaskell. She is currently working on a study of the construction of mid-Victorian popular culture.

PALO ALTO COLLEGE LRC
1400 W. VILLARET
SAN ANTONIO, TEXAS 78224-2499

WITHDRAWN

PALO ALTO COLLEGE LRC

3 6171 00116232 7